Byzantine Istanbul
A Self-Guided Tour

Robert van den Graven

Bosphorus
Golden Horn
Sea of Marmara
Taksim
Galata
Üsküdar
Galata Tower
Galata Bridge
Dolmabahçe Palace
Maiden's Tower
First Settlement
Goth's Column
Archeological Museum
Hagia Eirene
Hagia Sophia
Sultanahmet
Mosaic Museum
Great Palace Ruins
Bucolean Palace
SS. Sergius and Bachus
Hippodrome
Binbirdirek Cistern
Column of Constantine
Basilica Cistern
Valide Han
New Mosque
Spice Bazaar
Fire Tower
Kalender Mosque
Beyazit Mosque
Ruins of the Forum of Theodosias
St. Theodore
Aqueduct of Valens
Pantocrator Monastery
Pantepoptes Monastery
Gül Camii
Fatih Mosque
Cisterns of Asper
Patriarchate
Fethiye Mosque
Mary of the Mongols
Chora Church
Cisterns of Acitos
Edirne Gate
Tekfur Palace
Holy Well of Blachernae
Dungeons of Blachernae Palace
Topkapı Gate
Mevlevihane Gate
Cistern of Mocius
Spring of the Fishes
Silvri Gate
Belgrade Gate
St. John Stoudion
Golden Gate Yedikule
Key
Old Imperial Constantinople
Ottoman Monuments
Walls

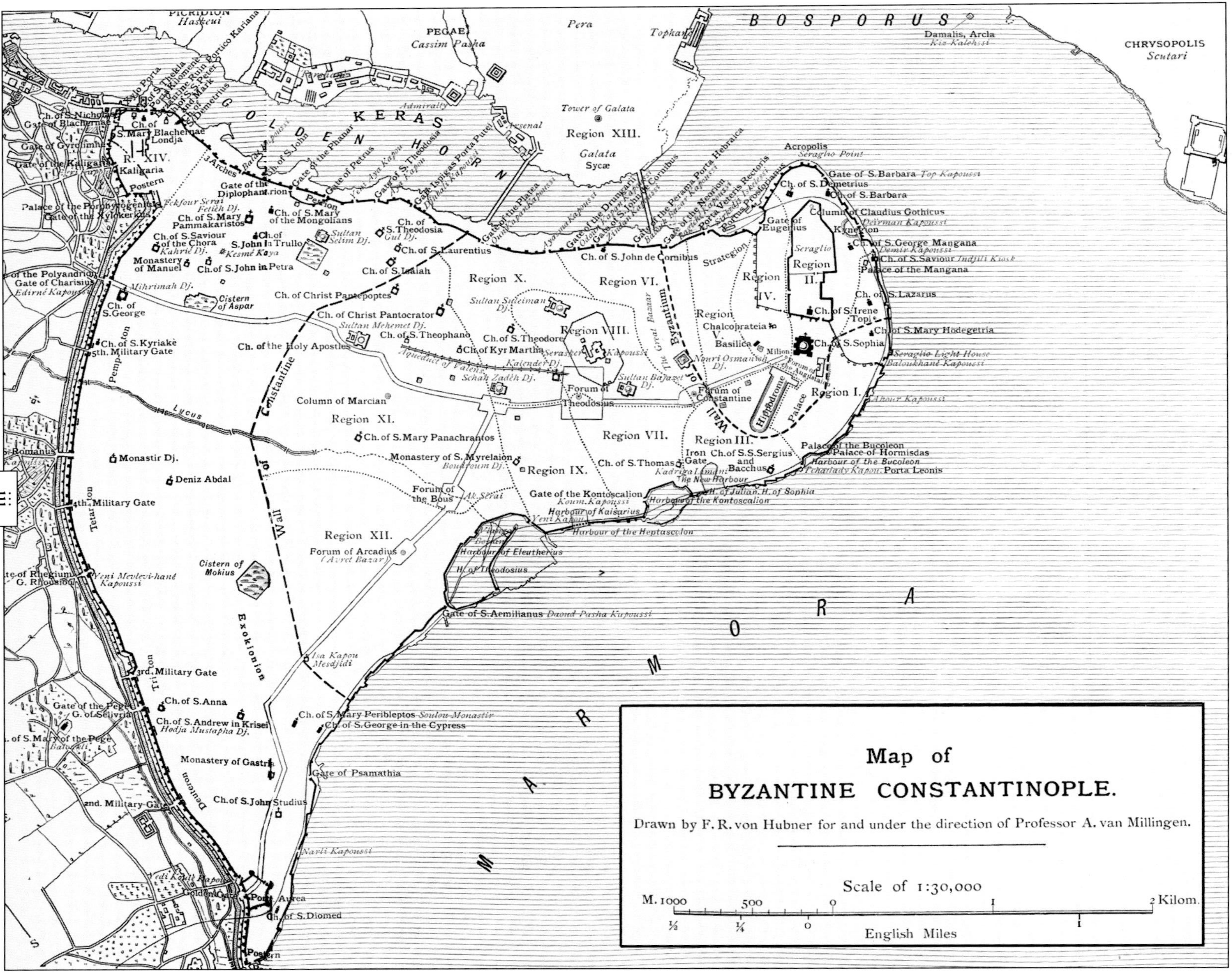
Map of
BYZANTINE CONSTANTINOPLE.
Drawn by F. R. von Hubner for and under the direction of Professor A. van Millingen.
Scale of 1:30,000
M. 1000 500 0 1 2 Kilom.
½ ¼ 0 1
English Miles
BOSPORUS
CHRYSOPOLIS
Scutari
Damalis, Arcla
Kiz Kalehssi
Pera
Tophane
PEGAE
Cassim Pasha
PICRIDION
Hasskeui
Tower of Galata
Region XIII.
Galata
Sycæ
Arsenal
Admiralty
KERAS
GOLDEN HORN
MARMORA
Acropolis
Seraglio Point
Gate of S. Barbara
Top Kapoussi
Ch. of S. Demetrius
Ch. of S. Barbara
Column of Claudius Gothicus
Gate of Eugenius
Kynegion
Ch. of S. George Mangana
Demir Kapoussi
Ch. of S. Saviour
Indjili Kiosk
Palace of the Mangana
Seraglio
Region II.
Region IV.
Ch. of S. Lazarus
Ch. of S. Irene
Topi
Ch. of S. Mary Hodegetria
Ch. of S. Sophia
Seraglio Light House
Baloukhané Kapoussi
Region I.
Ahour Kapoussi
Hippodrome
Palace
Milion
Forum of the Augustaion
Region V.
Chalcoprateia
Basilica
Strategion
Ch. of S. John de Cornibus
Byzantium Wall
Region VI.
The Great Bazaar
Nouri Osmanieh Dj.
Forum of Constantine
Region III.
Palace of the Bucoleon
Palace of Hormisdas
Harbour of the Bucoleon
Tchatlady Kapou.
Porta Leonis
Ch. of S.S. Sergius and Bacchus
Iron Gate
Kadriga Limani
The New Harbour
H. of Julian. H. of Sophia
Harbour of the Kontoscalion
Ch. of S. Thomas
Region VII.
Gate of the Kontoscalion
Koum. Kapoussi
Harbour of Kaisarius
Yeni Kapou
Harbour of the Heptascalon
Harbour of Eleutherius
H. of Theodosius
Gate of S. Aemilianus
Daoud Pasha Kapoussi
Region VIII.
Serasker Kapoussi
Sultan Bajazet Dj.
Forum of Theodosius
Region IX.
Region X.
Sultan Suleiman Dj.
Ch. of S. Theodore
Ch. of Kyr Martha
Kalender Dj.
Schah Zadeh Dj.
Aqueduct of Valens
Ch. of S. Theophano
Sultan Mehemet Dj.
Ch. of Christ Pantocrator
Ch. of Christ Pantepoptes
Ch. of S. Isaiah
Ch. of S. Laurentius
Ch. of S. Theodosia
Gul Dj.
Sultan Selim Dj.
Ch. of S. Mary of the Mongolians
Ch. of the Holy Apostles
Column of Marcian
Region XI.
Ch. of S. Mary Panachrantos
Monastery of S. Myrelaion
Bodroum Dj.
Forum of the Bous
Ak Serai
Region XII.
Forum of Arcadius
(Avret Bazar)
Constantine Wall
Isa Kapou Mesdjidi
Exokionion
Cistern of Mokius
Cistern of Aspar
Lycus
Ch. of S. Mary Peribleptos
Soulou-Monastir
Ch. of S. George in the Cypress
Gate of Psamathia
Monastery of Gastria
Ch. of S. John Studius
Narli Kapoussi
Porta Aurea
Ch. of S. Diomed
Golden Gate
Yedi Koulé Kapou
Postern
2nd. Military Gate
Deuteron
Ch. of S. Andrew in Krisei
Hodja Mustapha Dj.
Ch. of S. Anna
3rd. Military Gate
Triton
Gate of the Pege
G. of Selivria
Ch. of S. Mary of the Pege
Baloukli
Gate of Rhegium
G. Rhousion
Yeni Mevlevi-hané Kapoussi
4th. Military Gate
Tetarton
Deniz Abdal
Monastir Dj.
Romanus
5th. Military Gate
Ch. of S. Kyriaké
Pempton
Ch. of S. George
Gate of the Polyandrion
Gate of Charisius
Edirné Kapoussi
Mihrimah Dj.
Monastery of Manuel
Ch. of S. Saviour of the Chora
Kahrié Dj.
S. John in Trullo
Kesmé Kaya
Ch. of S. John in Petra
Ch. of S. Mary Pammakaristos
Fetieh Dj.
Tekfour Serai
Palace of the Porphyrogenitus
Gate of the Xylokerkus
Gate of the Diplophanarion
Petrion
Gate of Petrus
Gate of the Phanar
Gate of S. John
Balat Kapoussi
3 Arches
Postern
Kaligaria
R. XIV.
Ch. of S. Mary Blachernae
Londja
Gate of the Kaligaria
Gate of Gyrolimne
Gate of Blachernae
Ch. of S. Nicholas
Xylo Porta
Ch. of S. Thekla
Porta Kiomene
Gate of S. Theodosia
Aya Kapou
Gate Ispigas Porta PuteI
Gate of the Platea
Oun Kapan Kapoussi
Gate of the Drungarii
Gate of S. John de Cornibus
Gate of the Perama Porta Hebraica
Gate of the Neorion
Porta Veteris Rectoris
Portus Prosphorianus

Copyright © 2001 Robert van den Graven
All rights reserved. No portion of this book may be reproduced in any form without the written permission of the author.

Published by Çitlembik Publications
Şeyh Bender Sok. 18/5 Asmalımescit, Tünel
80050 Istanbul TURKEY
Web Page: http://www.citlembik.com.tr
E-Mail: kitap@citlembik.com.tr

Editing: Nancy Öztürk
Layout and Design: Tamia Lum

Every effort has been made to assure the accuracy of the contents of this book, however the author and publisher will accept no responsibility for, loss, accident, or inconvenience experienced as a consequence of unintentional misinformation.

Photo Credits:
Dumbarton Oaks, Washington, DC.: p. 87
Damla Çelikkol and Mustafa Kağan Hekim: p. 13 (top), Chora Church chapter (p.65-74), Cover (top left)
Tamia Lum: p. 14, p.37, p.81 (top and bottom right)
Robert van den Graven: All others

Çitlembik Publications

Contents

Map of Existing Byzantine Sites in Istanbul — ii
Map of Byzantine Constantinople — iii

Introduction: The Byzantine World — 1

The District of the Great Palace (map) — 17

    The Hagia Sophia (map) — 18

    The Hippodrome — 27

    The Great Palace — 33

    Hagia Eirene and the Palace Gardens — 39

The Byzantine 5th Avenue (map) — 43

    The Byzantine 5th Avenue — 44

    The Cisterns of the City — 47

The Land Walls (map) — 51

    From the Marble Tower to the Mevlevihane Kapı — 55

    From Edirnekapı to the Golden Horn — 60

    The Chora Church — 65

Fener (map) — 75

A Walk Through the Old Districts (map) — 83

Galata (map) — 91

The Bosphorus (map) — 95

Additional Byzantine Monuments and Useful Information — 103

Acknowledgments

Thanks to:

Helen Ostafew for the diligent work of correcting my English,
Miss Denizman of the Turkish Tourist Office in The Hague for her kind assistance,
My friend Ziya for providing nice gravures,
The Galata Residence Hotel for my pleasant stay in the heart of old Galata,
Tamia Lum for the fine job she has done in the lay-out of this book.

Last but not least, many thanks to Nancy for giving me the great opportunity to write a book on the city I love so much.

Robert van den Graven

The Byzantine World (330 - 1453)

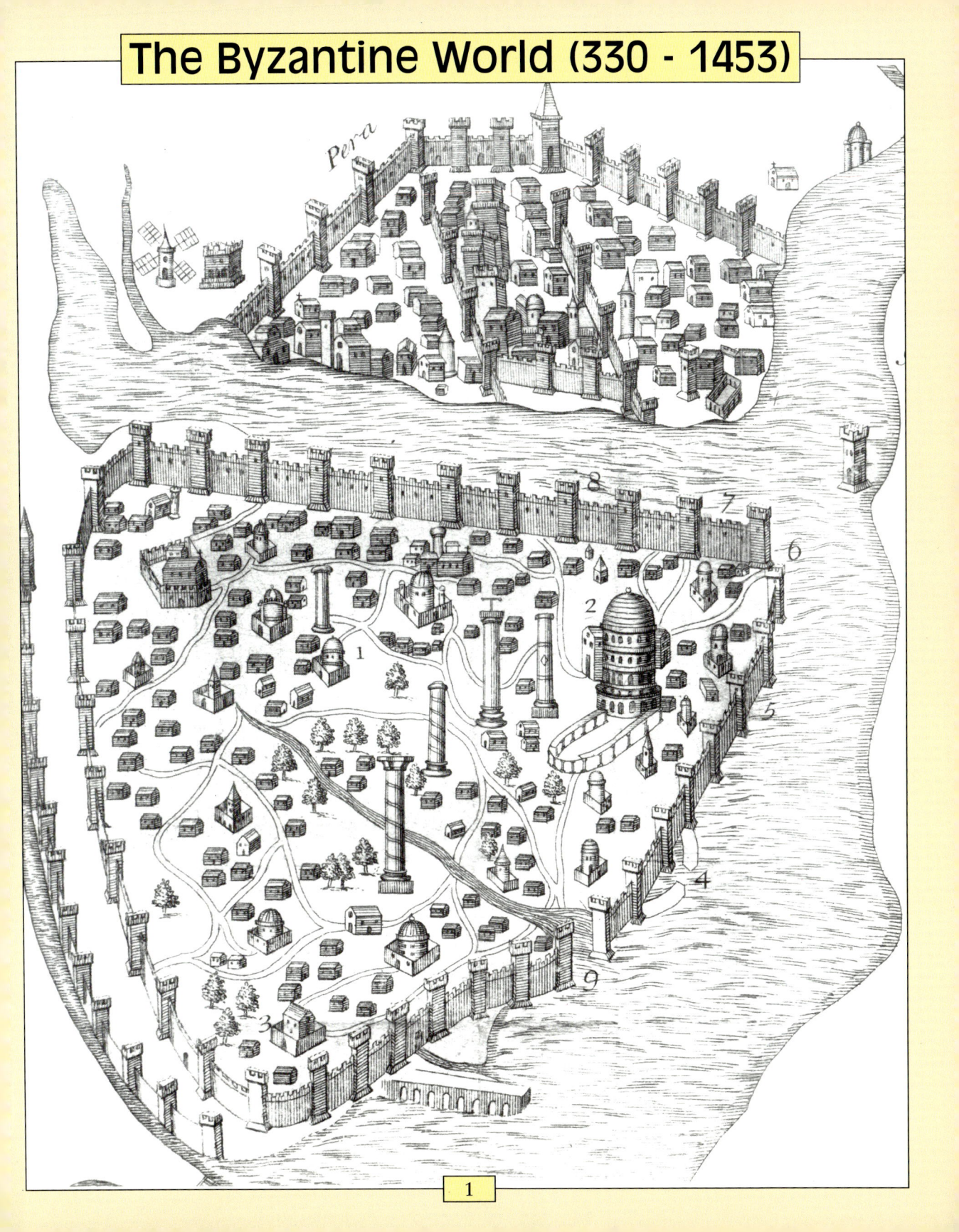

Constantinople

Constantinople was founded in that misty age when gods could be men and men could be gods. It is said that in the middle of the seventh century BC, a ruler named Byzans set off with a company of his countrymen in search of a site for a city. According to the oracle of Delphi it was to be founded "opposite the land of the blind." As his ship rounded the promontory where the Topkapı Palace now stands, he instantaneously knew what the oracle had meant. The earlier colonists who had settled in present-day Kadıköy, the ancient Chalcedon, must have been blind indeed to have disregarded the triangular peninsula opposite. First of all, the peninsula was surrounded by water on two sides making it easy to defend, and the Golden Horn, an inlet of the Bosphorus, was a natural harbor where ships could take shelter, even in the fiercest of storms. It was thus that the enterprising Greeks decided to build their city there, calling it Byzantion after their leader.

These were the humble beginnings of the New Rome, the mighty capital of the Byzantine Empire, and later that of the great Ottoman Empire. This book is a chronicle of late Roman and Byzantine times and a photographic essay of the splendors that have been left to us from more than a thousand years of history.

Who Were the Byzantines?

The Byzantines were Romans. The words "Byzantines" and "Byzantine Empire" as they are now commonly used were more or less invented by nineteenth century historians. The Byzantines thought of themselves as Romanoi and saw their Empire as the logical continuation of the Roman Empire in its legal, fiscal and administrative systems, and very appropriately called their capital the Nova Roma.

There was, however, one major difference between this new Roman Empire and the old: the Byzantine Empire was a Christian state. Bishop Eusebios formulated it this way. The Pax Romana, the peace that the Romans brought with them in the first two centuries A.D., had been instrumental to the Christian cause for it allowed the gospel to spread. Now that the Roman Empire was ruled by a Christian emperor, the role of Rome, where the inhabitants still adhered to their heathen ways, had ended and a new era had begun. The Byzantines were devout Christians, to a degree that would now verge on the incomprehensible. The Byzantines communicated with Christ, His mother, and the saints as if they were family members, and their Emperor was seen as God's living viceroy on earth. Processions were held almost nightly all around the city. Differences of dogma, which are now only the subject of tedious arguments by scholars, excited the masses, and the danger of enormous religious upheavals was always present in Byzantium. It was said that the city of Constantinople itself was under the divine protection of the Holy Mother of God, and her icon was carried around the walls during times of great danger. When the Slavs visited the city in the tenth century, they reported that in Byzantium God dwelled among the people.

Byzantine civilization, however, must also be understood from the aspect of its Greek inheritance. The Byzantines may have called themselves Romans, but at heart they were Greeks. Although this feature was not as dominant when the Empire was still an infant under Constantine the Great, a vast number of people of Constantinople spoke Greek, the lingua franca of the Empire. Greek learning also deeply influenced the church. The Gospels themselves had been written in Greek and the creed was formulated with the help of the categories of Greek philosophy.

Greek spirit was the virtual lifeblood of the Empire and its influence was phenomenal. The Byzantine gentleman was essentially a man of culture and learning. A good example is Theodore Metochites (1269-1332), the main contributor to the famous Chora Church (Kariye Mosque), a building that today ranks as one of the Byzantine highlights of present Istanbul. Metochites was a prolific author; he wrote commentaries on Aristotle and prided himself on his knowledge of ancient literature. Then there was Michael Psellus (1018-1096) who made his name teaching Platonic philosophy. He also pursued a successful career at court as the Grand Chamberlain. At the same time this leading intellectual of the Empire was accused of every Byzantine failing: lack of scruples, weakness, intrigue, servility and vanity—features that represent the more unpleasant sides of the Byzantine way. There could be no greater difference between these cultivated men and the men of the West, as the average Crusader was as bold as he was blunt. Westerners deeply distrusted the refined Greeks, with their subtle tongue and their heretic beliefs. At the same time—as so often is the case—they were envious of all the splendors of Byzantium.

The Capital of the Roman Empire

When Constantine chose to make Christianity the religion of his new Empire, he changed the course of history. It was a courageous step since the Gentiles at that time were vastly more numerous than the Christians, and his predecessor Emperor Diocletianus had still butchered them indiscriminately. Perhaps Constantine's belief played a role in selecting a fitting place for his new capital. Well-organized Christian communities were already in existence in many parts of present-day Turkey while they were much less strong in the West. Constantine must have realized that a new beginning was not going to be easy in ancient Rome.

Constantine was probably also moved by more prosaic motives. He had to curb the barbarians along the Danube while keeping a watchful eye on the Persian monarch. Constantinople proved to be an advantageous site because its location was on the verge of two continents. The Emperor set out on foot with a lance in his hand, to point out the line that was to be the boundary of his new capital. The growing circumference was observed with much astonishment by his following who declared that he had already far exceeded the usual size for a great city. "I shall still advance," replied the Emperor "till the invisible guide who marches before me, thinks proper to stop." After five years of construction the city was inaugurated on the 11th of May in 330 AD as the New Rome.

Nowadays there are no visible remains of Constantine's land walls, but we know that they began at the Golden Horn, and extended to the Sea of Marmara in a great circular arc. The city was then already five times as large as the Roman town that was scattered across the acropolis hill where the Topkapı Palace now stands. The awe-inspiring triple fortifications were built a hundred years later, making Constantinople the biggest metropolis in the world and an impregnable bastion of Christianity. Had it not been for these mighty land walls, the Arabs would have overrun Constantinople and the inheritance of the classical world would have probably been lost forever.

It is said that Constantinople was built on the fleecing of all other cities because by royal decree the cities of Greece and Asia were robbed of their most valuable works of art in order to adorn the streets and forums of the new capital.

It was Theodosius I (390), depicted on the marble base of the Egyptian Obelisk that he himself erected on the Hippodrome, who made Christianity the state religion and ordered heathen temples and shrines closed. The temples proved a good source of building material. Walking in the Yerebatan Cistern, the most famous of all city underground water reservoirs, we are confronted by the imposing heads of Medusa, taken from some temple.

Water supply was as great a problem for the city then as it is today. Cisterns were constructed and filled with water carried by aqueducts. A number of these can be found in the Belgrade Forest, but the best known is the picturesque aqueduct of Emperor Valens (364-78) in the center of town

4

The Capital of the Byzantine Empire

Most historians consider the time from Constantine the Great until the reign of Justinian in the sixth century AD as a transitional period. On the death of Theodosius I, the Roman Empire was divided between his two sons. Honorius took the Western Roman Empire and Arcadius took the Eastern. It was at that time that the inexorable decline started. Just eighty years later the Western Roman Empire was dead and after the fateful night of January 17, 395, when Rome was sacked by the Barbarians, Western Europe began its slide into the medieval age.

Emperor Justinian (527-65) was a man of boundless energy—ancient scribes refer to him as the Emperor who never slept—who worked day and night for the restoration of the Roman Empire. He held back the barbarians, managed to recapture Italy and laid the basis for law throughout the Empire. The Emperor's great ambitions had their shadows too, for they resulted in severe burdens of taxation and tremendous demands of manpower. It is no small wonder that the circus factions of the Hippodrome—who had virtually become political parties—joined together in the year 527 with the object of toppling the Emperor. After the ruthless suppression of the so-called Nika revolt, Justinian set out to rebuild his city on an even grander scale than before. Three of Justianian's churches in Istanbul survive: the church of the Hagia Sergius and Bacchus (know by the locals as Küçük (*little*) Aya Sofya), the Hagia Eirene (in the first courtyard of the Topkapı Palace) and, above all, the Hagia Sophia, one of the greatest buildings of the world, which symbolizes Byzantine power at its zenith.

Byzantine Art

Art also experienced a great change. In the days of Constantine the artist worked with the old forms to express a new Christian content. Now the artist found new unworldly forms. In the fourth century Christ could still be depicted as an agile young man, much like the radiant Apollo before Him. In the sixth century Christ had grown old, looking tired and gray, but this did not matter. From that time on the content mattered and the artist sought to depict the super human, not the ideal human form. The spirit of the spectator was to be uplifted to heaven and anything reminiscent of the world of the senses was not beneficial to that course: hence the unnatural colors (gold was the favorite), the immobile figures and the intense fixed gaze, betraying an inner life that the Roman artists had never wanted to convey.

The classical artist was not doomed to spend his days in idleness for his skills were still needed in the secular realm. We have a wonderful example of this in Constantinople. There has been a tiresome debate among scholars over the date of the great floor mosaic for the Great Palace. Since it was so perfectly classical, complete with pagan gods and mythological creatures, it was believed for many years that it could not be later than the fourth century, whereas in fact it has been recently dated as belonging without doubt to the reign of Justinian (6th century AD).

The Ages of Turmoil

After the strong reign of Justinian, Byzantine power dwindled significantly. The Western half of the Empire was lost as quickly as it had been gained, never again to be part of the Byzantine domain. In fact the Byzantines even found great difficulty in holding on to their beloved capital as the armies of the infidel were strong. Palestine, Syria and Egypt (one of the richest provinces of the Empire) fell rapidly into Islamic hands, and in 674 the Arabs launched their sea-borne siege of Constantinople. It was during this siege that Eyüp Ensari, the last companion of the Prophet, fell. His tomb is ranked among the holiest places of Islam and can still be visited today in the suburb of Eyüp outside the walls. In 678 the Arab fleet withdrew after having suffered severe losses. This occurred through the employment of a new and lethal weapon, the Greek fire, a flaming liquid that could not be extinguished by water.

Inwardly, the Empire was also divided. It had already seen enormous religious conflict about the nature of Christ and the divinity of the Virgin, but probably no struggle proved more destructive than the iconoclastic period (roughly from 717 until 843). The ban on images and relics was perhaps inspired by the formidable success of the Arab armies. Heated discussions had always arisen over whether or not it was sacrilege to clothe the divine in human garb. The saintly Eusebios rebuked the sister of Constantine for wanting to obtain an image of Christ. Now that the armies of the Arabic infidels were proving victorious on nearly all fronts, it was thought that their success might be attributed to the fact that they had ruthlessly banned all figural images. This idea was not lost on Leo III, who with his Syrian background was already affected by Islamic beliefs. In 726 the Emperor destroyed the largest and most prominent icon of Constantinople: the image of Christ above the Imperial Gate of the Great Palace. This resulted in nearly 125 years of bitter strife between the monks and the establishment. But since iconoclasm had always been more or less imposed on the people, and although the worship of images had always enjoyed widespread popularity, it inevitably had to come to an end. The final victory of the Holy Images in 843 is known as "The Triumph of Orthodoxy" and is still celebrated on the first Sunday in Lent. A quarter century later the first figurative mosaic, that of the Mother of Christ, was unveiled in the Hagia Sophia, and it can still be admired in the apse of the church today.

The Second Golden Age

When the Empire finally recovered in the ninth century, it was much reduced in size. Although the Byzantines still thought of themselves as being a superpower, in fact, they had already outplayed their role. The huge loss of territory, not only to Italy—whose occupation had been more a matter of prestige than anything else—but also to Egypt, Syria and Palestine, proved to be a blessing in disguise. The dominion that the Byzantines managed to hold on to was a mid-sized state, comprising only present-day Turkey, Greece and the Balkans. As such it was much easier to administer than the huge states of Byzantium that they had had to preside over in the past.

In a way Byzantium was a land of limitless possibilities, and its cultural influence reached far beyond the limits of its borders. Basil, an uneducated peasant boy from Thrace, managed to live the dream of Byzantium. Arriving in Constantinople as a penniless wanderer, he got a job at the Palace stables, and from there it took him just nine years to ascend to the throne. Emperor Basil I (867-86) was the founder of the Macedonian Dynasty, the only imperial family that lasted more than a few generations on the throne, and the resulting stability heralded an age of unexampled brilliance and strength which lasted until 1056. During that time Bulgaria was assimilated

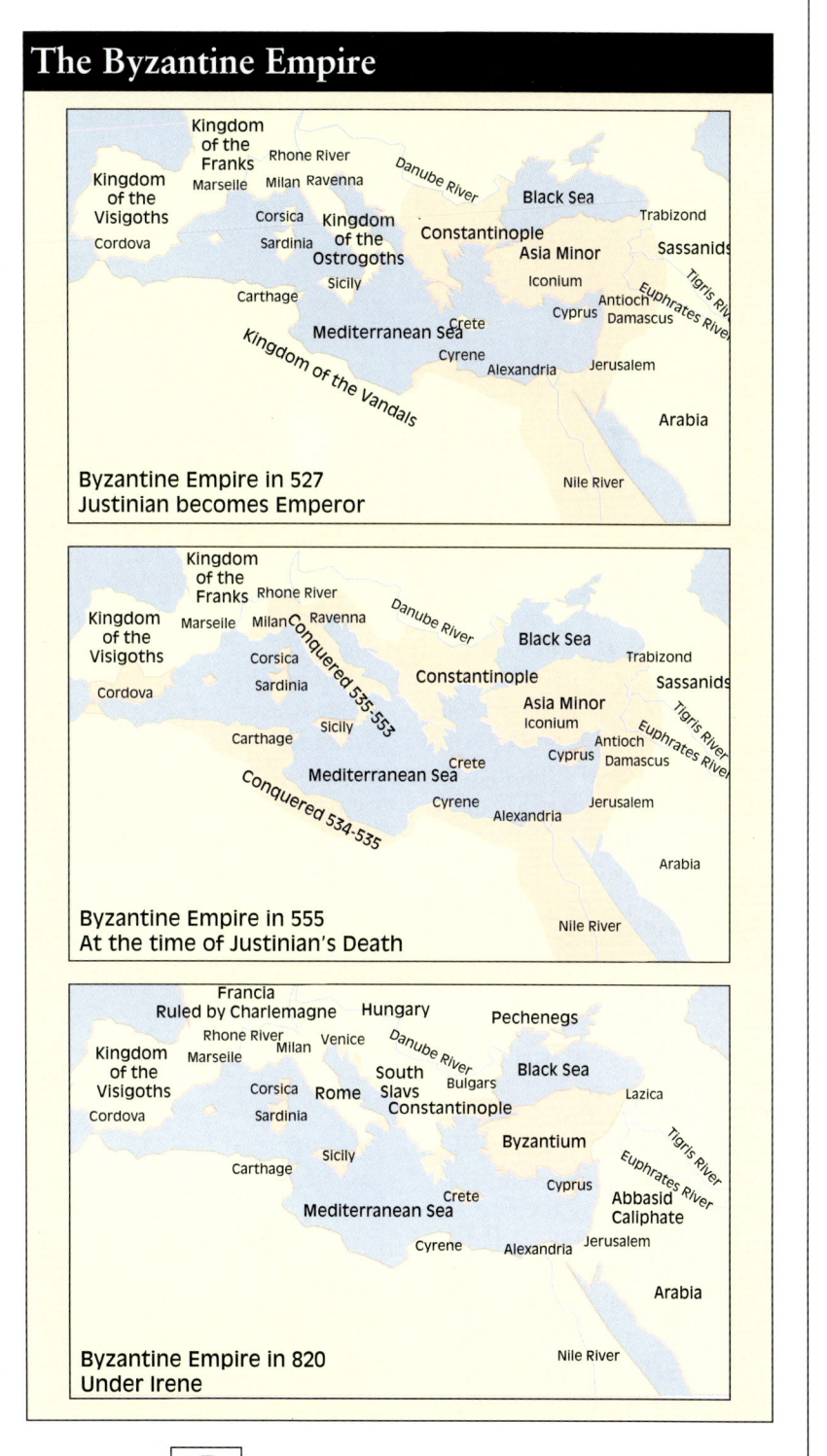

The Byzantine Empire

Byzantine Empire in 527
Justinian becomes Emperor

Byzantine Empire in 555
At the time of Justinian's Death

Byzantine Empire in 820
Under Irene

into the Empire and the ancient frontiers along the Danube were re-established. The Arabs took a beating too. Crete fell in 961, Cyprus four years later, and the important cities of Antioch and Edessa saw victorious Byzantine soldiers parading through their streets.

The conversion of the Slavs was to prove more important historically than the victories won on the battlefield. In the ninth century Cyril and Methodius, two Byzantine missionaries, set out to convert the Slavs. They invented the Cyrillic script so that the newly acquired faith of the Slavs could be written. In so doing they conveyed Byzantine literature and learning to the Balkans, giving them a brotherhood in faith and a Slavic literary language. A hundred years later the conversion of the Russians followed. In 988 Vladmir, Prince of Kiev, sent emissaries to Constantinople and inspired by the resplendent liturgy in the Hagia Sophia, *"for they knew not whether they were in heaven or earth,"* the prince was baptized in the cold waters of the Dnieper. Of course, ecclesiastical diplomacy of such scale brought the Byzantines in direct conflict with the other ecclesiastical power broker of that time, Rome. The Pope claimed that the power of the Church of Rome was universal, an idea the Byzantines were not prepared to grant. Not that they desired total rule, they only wanted to be regarded as equal, together with the other patriarchies. This led to the great schism of 1054, with both churches excommunicating the other.

During the Macedonian Dynasty, Constantinople was a very different city than it had been under Justinian. Constantinople in the tenth century was no longer a classical Roman city. The broad avenues, colonnaded streets and forums were supplanted by a maze-like grid of streets far removed from the mathematical planning of Roman towns. Another good example of the changing of times was the decline of the public bath. In Roman life nudity was not at all problematic and the sexes mingled freely. But in the course of time the body became shameful, a pool of muddy desires. The closing down in the ninth century of the Great Baths of Zeuzippos which Justinian had lovingly restored, meant the abandonment of the classical way of life. Instead of erecting public forums, monasteries were built at an amazing speed. The Pantocrator, an impressive monastery church—today the Zeyrek Mosque—still looms over the city, high on a ridge above the Golden Horn.

The Coming of the Turks and the Crusaders

The great Emperor Basil II (976-1025) was succeeded by a series of weak rulers. They failed to maintain adequate frontier defenses while straining the resources of the treasury to support ostentatious court rituals. The provincial aristocracy grew more powerful day-by-day as the government lost its grip on the Empire. The loyalty of this "noble" man to the court was feeble, and some even fought on the side of the infidels. The landlords harshly suppressed free farmers, the former backbone of the Byzantine forces, and corruption flowered on a scale never seen before. At court the wily and whimsical Empress Zoë reigned. Her surviving sister, the Empress Theodora, brought the Macedonian Dynasty to an inglorious end in 1056.

The Turks appeared on the stage during this period of great danger when the Empire was at its weakest. The Turkish pagan tribes were well known for their fighting skills and found it very easy to get employment with the Arab rulers. The Seljuks—the first Turkish tribe to write history—were recruited as mercenaries in the tenth century for the Caliph of Baghdad and quickly became devote Muslims. In 1055 they assumed control in Baghdad and in 1071 the Byzantine army and the Seljuk Turks clashed at Manzikert, near Lake Van in Eastern Turkey. The Byzantine army was destroyed and the Emperor himself captured. It was a shattering blow, for the Byzantines lost all of their eastern provinces.

The Byzantines soon had even more worries for an enemy was advancing in the West that was possibly even more dangerous. In the fateful year of 1071 the Norman adventurer Robert Guiscard seized Bari, the last Byzantine foothold in Italy.

Venice was also to play a major, and even decisive, role in the affairs of the Late Byzantine Empire. The Byzantine Emperor Alexius I Comnenus (1081-1118) had no great love of Venice, but he badly needed help against the Normans, and Venice was a good choice. The Venetians were powerful and the merchant republic was actually of Byzantine offspring; in her former years it had been nothing but a Byzantine colony on the mudflats. Nevertheless, Venice extracted heavy terms for help and demanded the exemption from trade customs throughout the Empire.

The Venetians fought the Normans in accordance with the agreement and the Byzantines seemed to have gained a powerful ally. However, in the years to come, it became all too clear that the long-term effects were less beneficial, for the loss of income due to trade concessions was enormous. The Byzantines even had to pawn their crown jewels to Venice.

All this occurred in the fourteenth century. For the moment the Empire was delivered from immediate danger due to the adroit maneuvers of Emperor Alexius, the founder of the Comnenian dynasty. They were to rule the Empire skillfully for a hundred years ensuring its sur-

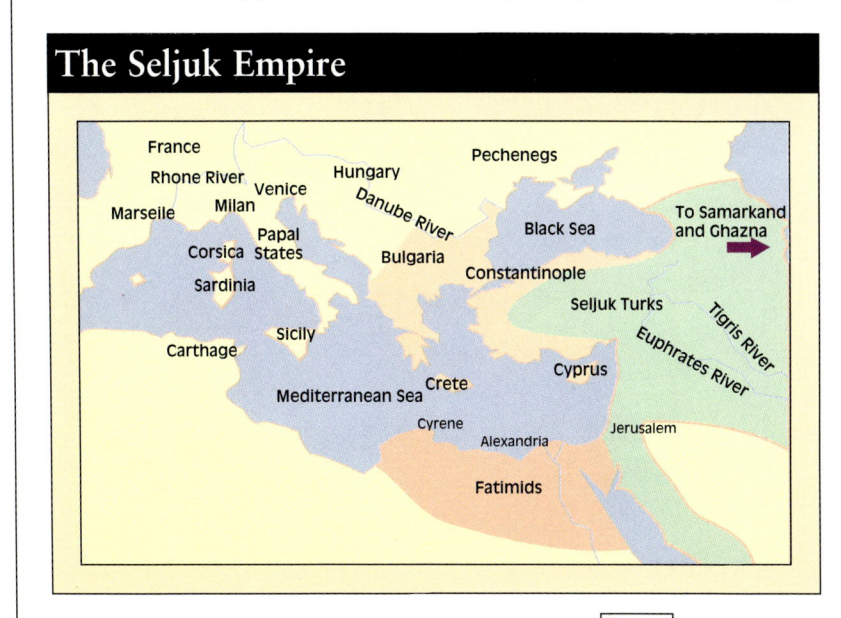

The Seljuk Empire

France
Rhone River
Venice
Marseille
Milan
Papal States
Corsica
Sardinia
Carthage
Sicily
Mediterranean Sea
Hungary
Danube River
Bulgaria
Pechenegs
Black Sea
Constantinople
Crete
Cyrene
Alexandria
Fatimids
Cyprus
Jerusalem
Seljuk Turks
Tigris River
Euphrates River
To Samarkand and Ghazna

vival in spite of seemingly insurmountable difficulties. Ironically enough, the "People of the Cross" presented one of these difficulties. In some ways Alexius was responsible for their arrival as he had asked Pope Urban II (1088-1099) for help in recovering his Asian provinces now that the Seljuk Turks were facing difficulties of their own. What the Emperor had in mind was a body of brave knights to aid him, not a horde of uncontrollable Crusader armies made up of the rabble of Europe.

With knights, peasants, women and children, driven by religious zeal, streaming, like tributaries joining a river, toward the capital, Alexius could do no more than make the best of the situation. He gave them food and shelter, showered them with gifts, and forced them to swear an oath of allegiance to him with their promise to restore all conquered territories to Byzantium. Actually the Emperor harbored no delusions regarding their fidelity, for Alexius knew very well that in spite of their lofty ideals of recovering the holy places from the infidel, they had no love for the Byzantines, whom they considered heretics. A hideous massacre followed the Crusaders' conquest of Jerusalem in 1099. This was a prefiguration of the fate that awaited Constantinople a little more than a hundred years later.

The Crusaders in the twelfth century had been unsuccessful in their war with the Muslims, but still had managed to set up a string of petty kingdoms from Antioch to Jerusalem (they were finally thrown out in 1291). Consequently Western hegemony in the eastern Mediterranean was firmly established at the expense of Byzantines. Constantinople saw a coming and going of the despised Crusaders—with their eyes firmly set on the wealth of the Byzantine—for over a hundred years. Since the Empire was in no shape to put up a good fight, the Emperor relied on that ultimate Byzantine weapon: diplomacy. Also concerned with the growing influence of Venice, the Emperors gave similar trade rights to the Pisans and Genoese. The Doges, of course, were not amused and more trouble was ahead, for an outbreak of hate against the foreigners in 1182 led to a massacre of Latin merchants in the city. As a result Venice had every reason to wish for the destruction of the Byzantine Empire.

John II, Irene and Alexius Comnenus

The portrait of John II Comnenus (1118-1143) together with his Hungarian wife Irene can still be seen in the south gallery of the Hagia Sophia. John was nicknamed "John the Good" because he didn't display any of the usual Byzantine shortcomings. These faces have something that makes them like real human beings, beginning with the broad, swarthy face of the Emperor. The high cheekbones and wide forehead of the Empress betray her foreign birth and the portrait of Alexius is most effective in conveying the melancholic and sickly appearance of a prince who died before he could take on the royal purple. Here we can see that the Byzantine artist was no longer satisfied with painting his usual impassive figures, and that feeling had gradually made its way back into a form of art that was now less self-confident and less super-human than before.

The Fourth Crusade

The Crusade of 1204 provided Venice with an opportunity to destroy the Byzantine Empire when Enrico Dandolo, the sly old Doge of Venice, devised a plan of diabolical proportions. The Crusaders initially planned to land in Egypt, allegedly the weakest point of the Muslim defense. Demanding advance payment, Venice rented out ships to the crusading forces. The Crusaders decided to keep secret the Egyptian destination, as many knights were only willing to go to the Holy Land. The devious Venetians made this a public secret. As a result many people did not turn up, and so the Crusaders did not have enough funds to pay for the trip. The Venetians then suggested that this might not be so bad if the Crusaders would give them a hand in conquering the port of Zara, which had recently become occupied by the King of Hungary. The Crusaders willingly agreed and sacked the Christian city of Zara, much to the disgust of the Pope. For Constantinople, the case proved to be different because heretics ruled that city.

A short time later, Philip of Swabia sent a letter in which he made it clear that Alexius III, the son of the Byzantine Emperor Isaac Angelus (1185-1195), had asked for help in restoring his father, then held captive in the dungeons of the Blachernae Palace, to the throne. The young prince solemnly promised that in return for his father's freedom he would finance the conquest of Egypt and that—of even more importance to the Pope—he would submit the Orthodox Church to the authority of Rome. Alexius III had thus given the enemies of the Empire a suitable excuse to do just what they had always wanted to do: conquer Constantinople.

When Alexius III was put on the throne of Byzantium, he discovered very quickly that there was no way in which he could keep the promises he had so rashly made. His own people were fiercely against any concession to Rome and the imperial treasury was empty. This came as no surprise to Enrico Dandolo who had already foreseen how the events would unfold. The Crusaders then decided to launch an attack on the city. On April 9, 1204 they succeeded in breaching the sea walls on the Golden Horn. An indescribable carnage followed and for three days there was an orgy of unrestrained looting. None of the Arab or Turkish conquerors had ever behaved that way, and these men even pretended to do so in the name of Christ.

Never had so much beauty and art been wantonly destroyed. It seemed that the Crusaders found a use for everything. Even the bronze plates adorning the obelisk of Constantine Porphygenetius in the Hippodrome were melted down. The Venetians took many works of art home. The most famous example of their booty is the Hippodrome horses of Lysippus that now adorn the San Marco Basilica.

The Crusaders' Latin Empire was doomed from the beginning. Scarcely born, it fell into an agony of spasms and soon the Latin "Empire" consisted of only the city proper. This made it relatively easy for the Greek general Michael VIII Palaeologues (1259-82) to drive them out again in 1261.

An Eyewitness Account

They smashed the holy images and hurled the sacred relics of the Martyrs into places I am ashamed to mention ... They brought horses and mules into the Great Church, the better to carry off the holy vessels and the engraved silver and gold that they had torn from the throne, and the pulpit and the doors ... A common harlot was enthroned in the Patriarch's chair to hurl insults at Christ; and she sang bawdy songs, and danced immodestly in the holy place ... nor was there any mercy shown to virtuous matrons, innocent maidens or even virgins consecrated to God ... In the streets, houses, churches there could be heard only cries and lamentations.

- Byzantine historian, Nicetas Choniates

The Last Flowering

Constantinople had a Byzantine Emperor again with Michael VIII, but the Empire was in a sadly truncated state. Surviving from the once glorious Empire, besides the capital and its immediate environs, were only the lands around Nicea (Iznik) and Bursa in Western Turkey, and the greater part of Thrace, with the important cities of Adrianople (Edirne) and Thessalonica and a few Aegean islands. The city itself had been very badly ruined. The Great Palace was in such a sad state of repair that the Emperor moved his imperial household to the smaller Blachernae Palace. Many quarters of the city were deserted becoming gardens, olive orchards, fields of corn and wasteland. Within the walls lived perhaps some 50,000 people, whereas in the time of Justinian there had been more than half a million.

In spite of the internal strife and numerous outside threats from all directions, under Palaeologan rule the tottering Empire showed itself capable of brilliant feats in the intellectual and cultural field. The south gallery of the Hagia Sophia is still adorned with one of the finest works of art of that period: the mosaic panel of Deesis (late 13th century) with St. John the Baptist and the Mother of God pleading for the salvation of mankind. The mosaic demonstrates the development of art in the Late Byzantine period. In the twelfth century mosaic of John Comnenus and Irene there is a hint of the emergence of a new more humanistic style. In the Deesis panel this style is blossoming. Here Christ is no longer conceived as the Pantocrator, the Omnipotent, but as Jesus the man, compassionate, and even melancholy. There can be no greater difference than that found between this figure and the impassive and majestic Christ (end of ninth century) that gazes down at us from above the imperial doorway in the narthex of the Hagia Sophia.

Palaeologan artists were great storytellers. The walls of the Kariye Mosque or Chora Church are covered with early fourteenth century mosaics that depict the story of the childhood of the Virgin and that of the Incarnation. This was a new development as the mosaics and frescoes of earlier days were executed on a much more monumental scale. Of course there were small icons then too, but their effect was to be mystical, providing the right atmosphere for communicating with the divine. The artists of the Chora Church wanted to make their church one big picture book, providing more information for illiterate onlookers.

This was also a time of fierce intellectual debate. We have

already mentioned Theodore Metochites, the main contributor to the Chora Church. He had many colleagues, the greatest of whom was the Greek philosopher George Gemistus Plethon, founder of a neo-Platonic academy. This man was so influenced by Greek heritage that he offended even his fellow Christians by frequently referring to God as Zeus and talking of "the gods" in the plural. The rebirth of Greece was Plethon's political objective. The Empire, after all, had shrunk now to the lands that were traditionally Greek and the intellectuals, painfully aware that their beloved New Rome was dying, sought comfort from their Greek ancestors. As a consequence, in the fourteenth century Byzantines suddenly began to speak of themselves as Hellenes. This was an unprecedented event. To admire Greek learning was one thing, to say that the Emperor was ruler of Greeks was another. This meant the denial of the ecumenical idea, that there could only be one Emperor in the world for all true believers, as there could be only one God in heaven. In the past an ambassador had nearly been driven away from the Palace when he addressed the Emperor as "King of the Greeks."

The End of an Empire

By the end of the thirteenth century Asia Minor was in a state of anarchy. The Mongols, under the leadership of the infamous Genghis Khan, had effectively wiped the Seljuk State from the map and Anatolia was now a mosaic of little emirates. One of these emirates was ruled by Osman, whose name is pronounced Othman in Arabic, hence we speak of Ottoman. Although in the beginning not much more than a simple highwayman, Osman did remarkably well; after all, his domain was on the frontier of Byzantium, and so holy warriors poured in from all sides to fight the enemies of the Prophet. In 1304 the Ottomans reached the Marmara Sea and occupied the entire Asian side of present-day Istanbul.

Osman's son Orhan took Bursa in 1326 and made it their first capital city. After conquering some of the western parts of Asia Minor, the Turks crossed the Dardanelles in 1350. In 1361 Edirne was made the new capital, and from here the conquest of the Balkans was planned. The rope around the capital was becoming tighter by the day, as the city was now totally surrounded by Turks. At this time the Turks were able to dictate what the Byzantine emperors could and could not do. The daughters of the Byzantines were married to the sons of the Turkish sultan and sometimes the Byzantines even fought alongside the Turks. The Emperor of the Greeks had now become a mere vassal of his Turkish overlord. The city would have fallen then had it not been for the Mongols who once more rampaged through Asia and even captured the Ottoman Sultan Beyazıt (1402). Since, however, the Mongol objective was plunder and not the foundation of an empire, the Turks had time to recuperate.

The Byzantines used the respite to look for aid. John VIII was desperate and prepared to do anything to save the Empire. Eventually a union with Rome came about in 1439, but many Byzantines thought it better to be under the rule of the turban of the Turk than the tiara of the Pope. After all, Christ himself had distinguished between that which was Caesar's and that which was God's. In the earlier days the church had only defied authority when the Emperor had meddled with Christian beliefs, but the Turks had made no such demands and left the Christians in peace as long as they behaved like good citizens. From this point of view, Ottoman dominion was not particularly bad.

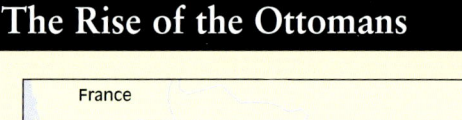

The Rise of the Ottomans

Map showing the Byzantine Empire in 1451 and The Ottomans, with locations including France, Rhone River, Milan, Venice, Marseille, Corsica, Sardinia, Sicily, Carthage, Crete, Mediterranean Sea, Cyrene, Danube River, Black Sea, Constantinople, Cyprus, Tigris River, Euphrates River, Jerusalem, Mamelukes.

The Conquest of Constantinople

The death struggle for the old Empire began with the ascent of the young and victorious Sultan Mehmet II (1451-1481) to the Ottoman throne. After Mehmet broke off diplomatic relations with the Byzantines, the Sultan set thousands of masons and laborers to work in the spring of 1452, building a fortress on the European shore of the Bosphorus. This site was directly opposite the Turkish fort of Anadolu Hisarı, constructed by his grandfather Beyazıt in 1394. After four months it was finished and was called Rumeli Hisarı (Roman Fortress) by the Turks. It still has its commanding position on the Bosphorus with canons that could effectively control the strait.

Now that the last life artery of the capital was choked, the siege could begin. There was still opposition in Mehmet's own circle of advisors as to whether or not Constantinople should be taken. Mehmet assured them that as long as Byzantium was alive it formed a threat, no matter how small and insignificant it might seem. Its people were cunning to the extreme and as Christians they could still count on the help of their fellow brothers in Europe. The house of Ottoman would never be safe with the walls of Constantinople still standing.

Easter is the most joyful event of the year for the Orthodox Church. The siege of Constantinople began that year on April 6, at a time when the hard winter was over and the land around the city was in bloom. Inside the walls, a frightened population awaited the events to come, for they knew that the reign of the Antichrist was at hand. The tent of the Sultan was placed opposite the gate of St. Romanus (Topkapı), considered the most vulnerable stretch of the walls. Most of the Sultan's cannons were consequently placed here, but in spite of their united firepower his troops were not able to drive out the defenders. The Sultan grew even wearier when another disaster struck. The entrance to the Golden Horn was defended by an impenetrable chain (on display today in the Istanbul Naval Museum) and when the hastily built Ottoman navy tried to break it, their ships were immediately sunk by the vastly superior imperial vessels.

The obstinate Sultan then conceived a bold plan to gain access to the Golden Horn. He transported his lighter vessels overland into the Golden Horn. This was not an easy feat since they had to be dragged over the hills. At Tophane the ships were taken out of the water and then they found their way back in the water at Kasımpaşa, slightly upstream. The Sultan now also threatened the walls near Fener and Balat. This necessitated the manning of the sea wall even though the Byzantines had scarcely enough people for the defense of the land walls. But they were determined not to surrender. By the end of May some Turkish generals were beginning to cast doubt on the whole enterprise. The siege had already lasted seven weeks, and although they outnumbered the Byzantines by far, and in spite of enormous firepower, the walls had yet to be breached. Worse still, it was possible that aid from the West might appear at any moment.

Mehmet IV knew that it was now or never. On the 27th of May he decided to address his troops. *"The city and the buildings are mine,"* said the Sultan, *"but I resign to your valour the captives and the spoil, the treasures of gold and beauty, be rich and happy."* The next day, a Monday, was to be a day of rest and penitence. On Tuesday the final attack from all sides was to begin. When the citizens woke up on that Monday, an eerie silence was noticed from the Turkish camp. It was clear to them what that meant. As the setting sun glinted on the cross of the Hagia Sophia, the Emperor and his suite went to mass, and together with his subjects he prayed for deliverance, with the cathedral resounding with cries and lamentations. The Emperor Constantine XI Palaeologus then summoned his commanders for the last time. He thanked everyone for their help, begged forgiveness of all he might have offended, and vainly attempted to infuse the hope which was already extinguished in himself. Toward midnight he rode to the Palace at Blachernae to take his place at the walls. He was never seen again.

In the early morning, the Bashibazouks were the first to attack. They were an untrained band of irregulars whose only importance for the Sultan was that they would sap the enemy's strength. They were no match for the well-trained Italian soldiers from Genoa, and before long their bodies started to fill the moat. The second wave of attack was formed by the disciplined troops of Anatolian Turks, but they too were driven back before the eyes of the outraged Sultan. Mehmet knew that now was the time, after half a day of fighting, to send his crack troops into battle, the Janissaries. Accompanied by their fearful music of drums and horns they attacked. Again resistance was fiercer than the Sultan had expected, but the end came with the wounding of the Italian commander of the elite force defending the walls. The Turks poured into the breaches of the wall and a troop of irregulars managed to climb one of the towers through a small insecurely bolted door in the wall. Seeing the Turkish flag now high above the city, the population fled in panic, hoping that at the very last moment an angel would come from heaven, spreading fire and destruction on the Turks.

Although Mehmet had promised three days of unrestrained looting, he ended it the very same day. Mehmet was not a monster, even though Christian historians liked to depict him that way. The Great Church made such an impression on the young Sultan that he decided to make it the chief mosque of his glorious city. Twenty-one years old, Mehmet IV had reached his goal. The last Byzantine Emperor had died fighting on the walls, and an era was thereby ended. Constantinople itself did not die for it would soon assume its old role under new masters. The next great chapter in its history had begun.

The District of the Great Palace

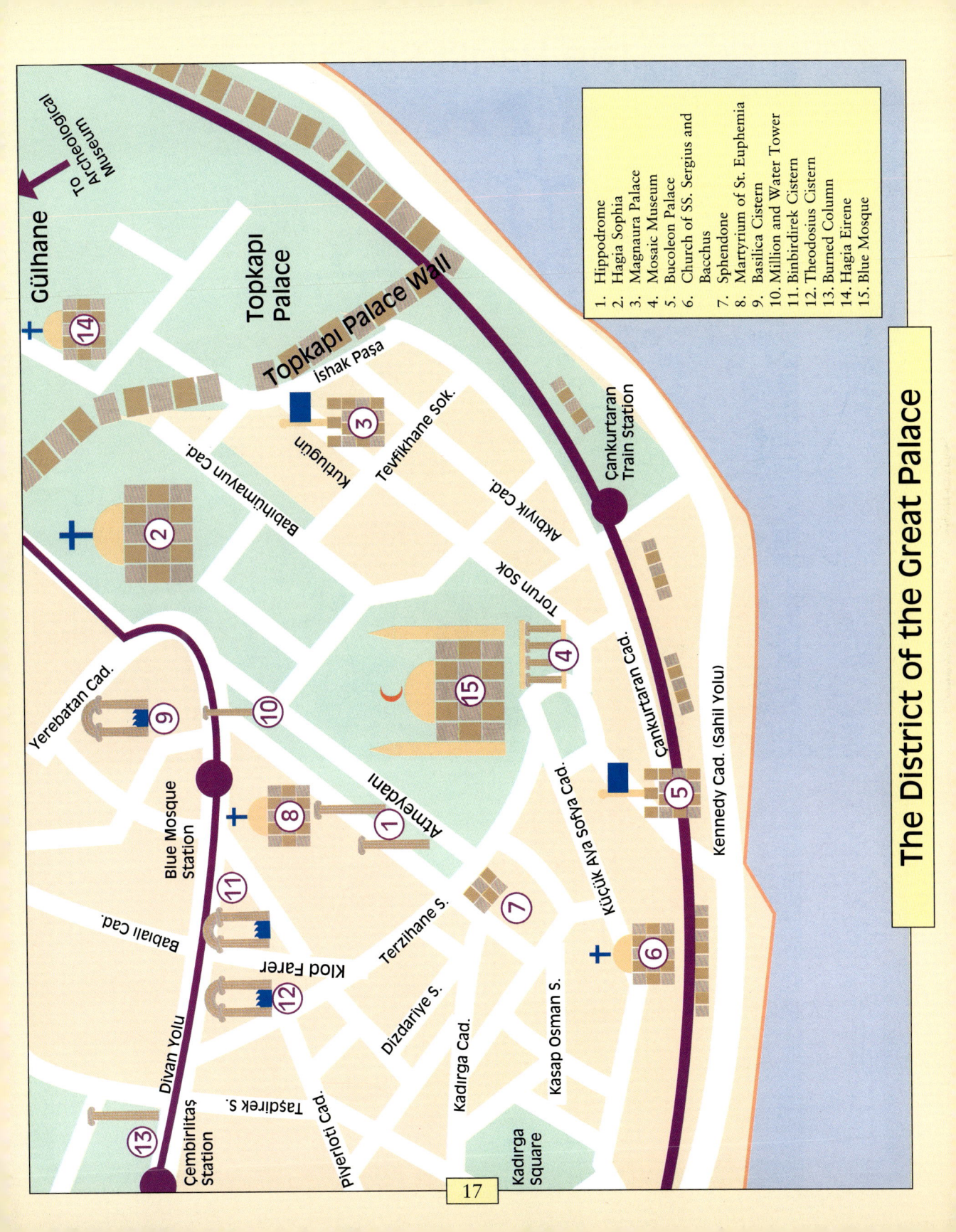

1. Hippodrome
2. Hagia Sophia
3. Magnaura Palace
4. Mosaic Museum
5. Bucoleon Palace
6. Church of SS. Sergius and Bacchus
7. Sphendone
8. Martyrium of St. Euphemia
9. Basilica Cistern
10. Million and Water Tower
11. Binbirdirek Cistern
12. Theodosius Cistern
13. Burned Column
14. Hagia Eirene
15. Blue Mosque

17

The Hagia Sophia

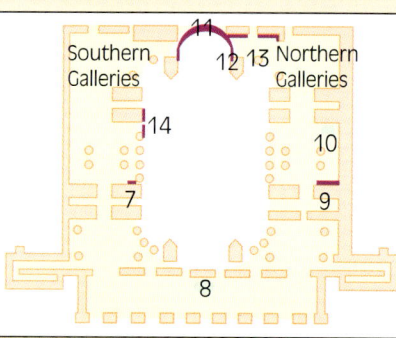

1. Entrance
2. Leo Mosaic
3. Altar and Cross Mosaic
4. Weeping Column
5. Marble Pavement
6. Dolphins
7. Alexander Mosaic
8. Empresses throne
9. Deesis Mosaic
10. Dandalo's Grave
11. Mary and Christ Mosaic
12. Gabriel Mosaic
13. Comnenus and Zoe Mosaics
14. Patriarch Mosaics
15. Mary, Justinian and Constantine

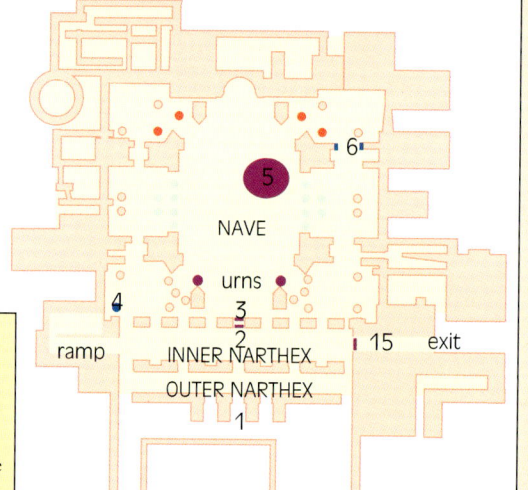

A Bit of History

The most venerable monument of Istanbul is the Church of Divine Wisdom, the Hagia Sophia. This is one of the greatest buildings of the world. Throughout its checkered history the Hagia Sophia has always made a huge impression on anyone entering it. The young Sultan was so impressed by the skill of its builders and the height of the dome that on the very day of the conquest he decided to convert the church into a mosque. However in spite of these recommendations, many people express disappointment once they see the Hagia Sophia. Its exterior is heavy and squat and the interior by far not as luminous as some of the postcards suggest. So they tend to agree with Mark Twain who called it "the rustiest old barn in heathendom." Atatürk ordained in 1935 that the Hagia Sophia should open its doors as a museum.

The Byzantine chronicler Procopius says that the church "rises in height to the very heavens and overtops the neighboring buildings like a ship anchored among them, appearing above the rest of the city, which it adorns and forms part of it." This is still true because the Hagia Sophia is visible from every spot in Istanbul as it looms over the city. The Hagia Sophia expresses the Empire's power at its zenith. At the same time, the building with its soaring dome was the ultimate symbol of the Orthodox faith, the place where the believers, touched by beauty, were uplifted to heaven.

The Hagia Sophia withstood all the earthquakes that have devastated the city, and it is nothing short of miraculous that up to this very day the delicately poised construction of the church should only have required minor restorations. If we ignore the four minarets that were added at various times after the Conquest, the domed mausoleums of several sultans and the unsightly buttresses, we have the church of Justinian in front of us.

The idea that Christians at the time of Constantine emerged from the catacombs like cave dwellers may be romantic, but is also rather foolish. There were already large Christian communities in the cities, but since prudence dictated that it was better to behave inconspicuously, they gathered in houses. When the Christians could finally confess their faith in the open, they needed a communal place of great size. Obviously the temple was not suitable, but the big utilitarian Roman buildings, such as the market hall or senate house, were quite useful, being simple rectangular buildings. The only significant change that the Christians made was that they placed the entrance at the short vertical side. This created the effect of a pathway. The believer had to walk down the aisle, toward the altar, leaving behind the material world and entering the spiritual realm. The earlier churches were sober buildings and none as sumptuous as the Hagia Sophia.

That no mention is made of the Basilica of Constantine that was consecrated in 360 may imply that there was nothing to get really excited about. The second church of Theodosius built in 415 had the same form and it shared the same fate as its predecessor since it was burned during the famous Nika-rebellion. The uprising was an unfortunate event, but it enabled the Emperor to set out to build a church that would surpass the Temple of Solomon. The building started within six weeks after the destruction of the old church and continued for five years, eleven months and ten days. The solemn inauguration took place on December 26, 537. Legend has it that on this occasion Justinian lost his imperial dignity for a moment, and raised his arms to heaven exclaiming "O Solomon I have outdone thee!"

Anthimenus of Tralles and Isidorus of Miletus were both academics of their craft and not just masterbuilders who knew from experience what could be done. Isidorus was a professor of mechanics and Anthemius a mathematician. Together the two men created a design that was unprecedented in architectural history. They understood that the traditional appearance of the basilica made it unsuitable as an expression of imperial ambition and greatness. The great vaulted structures of Old Rome, such as the domed pagan Pantheon, were actually more suitable in this sense, but they were not very functional for mass gatherings. Therefore the architects combined the best of both worlds. Covering a round building with a dome is a comparatively easy matter, but crowning a rectangular or square building with a dome presents a formidable challenge. This could only have been solved by minds who were capable of highly abstract thinking.

The Entrance and the Narthexes

Today we enter the church through the garden which occupies the site of the sixth century atrium. Scattered around are fragments of columns and capitals of pre-Justinian basilica. There is also an *ambo*, the reader's desk that stood in the center of the church. The meager remains of the fifth century basilica can be seen before the entrance.

The outer narthex is devoid of decoration. A dusty collection of fragments of mosaic floors found all around Istanbul are "exhibited" here. Let us reflect for a moment on the function of the narthexes in Byzantine liturgy. The celebration of the mass consisted of two clearly distinct parts. First there was the Ministry of the Word (readings and sermons) that those not yet baptized (the catechumens) could attend for instruction in the Faith. Those who were merely interested were allowed to listen to the readings from the narthex. The penitents, who stood outside in the atrium, were appropriately described as the "weepers." The Eucharist proper was only for the initiates. Following the reading of the Holy Gospel, the catechumens were dismissed and the doors of the nave were closed. Today, everyone is free to attend Orthodox services, but the call for the closing of the doors is still a part of the ceremony.

The inner narthex is of dazzling beauty. The walls are sheathed in colored marbles and the vaults are covered in gold-ground mosaic. These are decorated with stars and other geometrical designs, which according to a Byzantine poet, *"resembled the midday sun in spring gilding the mountain heights."* These mosaics stem from the time of Justinian, and it is most likely that all the original mosaics in the church were non-figural. A possible reason for this might be that space, form and light were felt to speak for themselves. The Byzantine theology after all was one of light and it was light that was to bring the cold fabric of stones to life. On the walls there are rare marbles from the four corners of the Empire. The wall plating is arranged with a delightful variety in size, and in the alternate placing of light against dark to give a sense of lightness and movement to the building.

The nine huge narthex doors, sheathed in bronze, give entrance to the nave. The tallest of them is the imperial door. Its importance is further emphazised by a bronze cornice, in the middle of which is a relief decoration of a throne, with the Gospel of St. John and a dove as a symbol of the Holy Spirit. The restless feet of the gatekeepers during endless Orthodox services brought about the depressions in the floor on either side of the doors. A tenth century mosaic depicting Christ is in the lunette above. On either side are roundels, one bearing the Virgin and the other the head of an angel.

At the beginning of the narthex lies the so-called Vestibule of the Warriors. Here the Emperor removed his sword and crown before entering the narthex. Above the door there is a beautiful tenth century mosaic depicting Emperor Constantine offering a model of Constantinople to the Mother of God while Justinian is offering a model for the great church. Don't forget to pay attention to the beautiful bronze temple doors from the first century BC.

An Emperor in Despair

The evidence dating the mosaic to the reign of Emperor Leo VI the Wise (886-912) is very amusing. The attitude that the Emperor assumes is one of extreme reverence and self-abasement, known as *proskynesis*. Yet in this case piety might not be the sole reason why the Emperor is groveling before Christ.

As a young prince Leo married a very pious wife who displayed a religious zeal that was considered to be extreme even by Byzantine standards. She forsook the pleasures of the imperial bed, preferring a rough mat in a corner, from which she rose every hour to pray. This presented a huge problem for Leo who desperately wanted an heir to the throne. When she passed away, the Emperor rejoiced and took his mistress Zoë to be his wife, but she also died leaving only a daughter. The unfortunate Emperor had to start all over again and worse still, a third marriage was frowned upon by the clergy who saw it as "moderated fornication." In the end the Emperor got his way, but when the new princess died giving birth to a dying baby prince, he must have felt cursed. Nevertheless Leo soon married again in his desire to propagate the dynasty and eventually got his much-desired son. This time the church revolted, for a fourth marriage was considered an unspeakable sin. So when Leo came to the Hagia Sophia, he was denied access. After much Byzantine diplomacy and intrigue, the marriage, sinful as it might be, was reluctantly recognized, but the Emperor was from then on only admitted to the Great Church as a penitent and was forbidden to sit at any time during the service.

The Nave

The basilica created the effect of a pathway. The Great Church conveys a different feeling, for eyes are irresistibly drawn up to the dome as soon as the threshold is crossed. This is the symbol of heaven, further walking is unthinkable. An atmosphere of contemplation is evoked as the spirit is transported to another dimension of being. The lengthening of the nave with two huge half-domes enhances the effect of the dome, because now, as in some other churches, the neck does not have to be craned to see it.

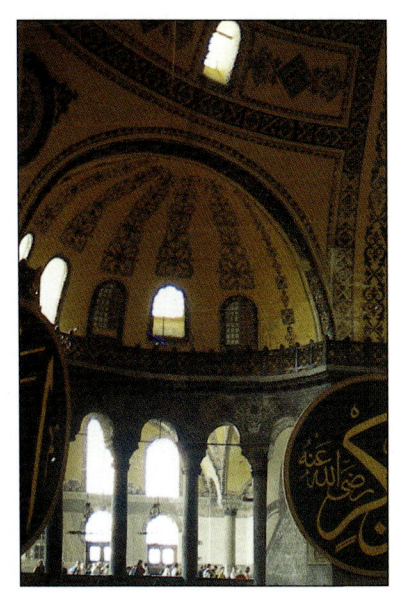

Four gigantic stone piers are used to crown the square building with a dome. These piers stand in a square and are sumptuously covered with marble. From each pier rise four arches. Empty triangular spaces exist at the points where the arches bend away from each other, breaking the continuity of the lines of the square summit. To make it continuous and circular the architects filled the triangular spaces with masonry to level the heads of the arches. This results in curved triangular surfaces called *pendentives*. They are easily recognized for each one is adorned with a six-winged cherub with faces covered with a star. (Those in the western pendentives are painted imitations.) In this manner the square summit is transformed into a circle. While the advantages of a basilica are retained, since the church still has the threefold division into nave and aisles, the splendid dome brings the Light of the Heavens to the otherwise gloomy looking building.

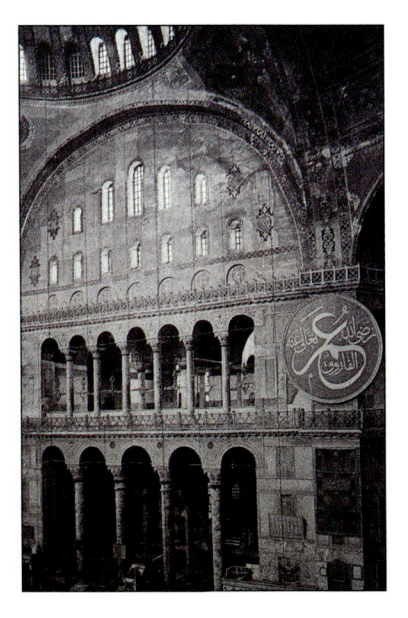

Originally the cupola was decorated with an image of Christ the Pantocrator (Omnipotent). In Ottoman times this image was replaced with an inscription of the famous Koranic verse, Nur (Light). The dome rises 56 meters above floor level with a width of roughly 30 meters. In comparison, the dome of the Blue Mosque is 23.5 meters in diameter and 43 meters high. One of the wonders of the newly erected church was the shallowness of its dome. It stood on a low drum pierced with windows, and looked, *"as though it were suspended from heaven by a golden chain."* The pressure of so low a dome, however, was great, and in 558 it came roaring down after an earthquake had weakened the structure. Isidorus the Younger, nephew of the deceased Isidorus, realized the audacity of the undertaking and made the dome somewhat higher than before, thereby lessening its outward thrust. Although there were two partial collapses in the years 989 and 1346, the present structure is essentially the same in design and partly in structure as that of Isidorus the Younger.

During Ottoman times the interior of the church was, of course, adapted to meet the needs of the Islamic faith, but the building itself underwent little change. The first additions were naturally a *mihrab* and *mimbar*. There were also marble tribunes placed for the chanters of the Koran. Noteworthy are the big Hellenistic alabaster urns which allegedly came from ancient Pergamum (now Bergama). The chandeliers with their countless small oil lamps are also

Ottoman. In the south nave there is a little library (1739). In the mid-nineteenth century the Italian brothers Fossati did some additional furnishing when the Hagia Sophia underwent a much-needed restoration. The sultan's loge to the left of the apse was then built and regrettably eight obtrusive shields were hung on the walls, bearing the names of Allah, the Prophet Mohammed and the first caliphs.

Most of the non-figural mosaic decorated dome is intact and patches of mosaic survive on the vaults, especially between the columns. All the other decorations seen today are actually crudely stenciled imitations of the gold-ground mosaic by the Fossati brothers. The mosaic tesserae were cut from glass, with gold leaf or other color applied to the back. The mosaic of the Holy Mother and Child (865) in the apse was the first after the iconoclastic struggle to appear in the Hagia Sophia. On the bottom of the arches flanking the apse, we see on the right Archangel Gabriel while on the left only a few sad feathers of Archangel Michael remain. In the north tympanum wall there are a number of niches toward the left. Three of them depict sainted patriarchs of the church (10th century).

Stonework of the Hagia Sophia

Many believe that the columns in the nave came from the Temple of the Sun at Heliopolis and that the dome was made of special bricks that were so light that twelve of them weighed no more than one normal brick. These charming tales originated from an unknown author from the eleventh century. This man invented entertaining stories, just as tourist guides do today. In contrast we have reliable accounts of eye-witnesses who tell us that the eight green marble columns of the nave came from Thessaly in Greece, whereas the soft white columns in the galleries were hewn from the famous quarries at the Island of Marmara (Proconnesus), not far from Istanbul. The same material was used for the capitals, the door frames, window lattices and other structural parts. The only columns that may have come from ancient buildings are the beautiful red porphyry columns of the exedra, the half round niches, at the four corners of the nave. This type of marble is found in Egypt and so must have been quarried there at some point in time.

Many columns have bronze collars to prevent them from bursting. There is one more column of interest: the so-called "weeping column." For centuries pilgrims have dipped a finger into the cavity in the column to be cured of fertility problems. It seems to be as popular today as it was then since there is always a throng of people in front of it with only one thing in mind.

The columns have delicately carved capitals. The original Roman acanthus leaf designs are so stylized here that they look more like lace. Inset on medallions are monograms of Justinian or Theodora. No two are quite identical.

There are other pieces of beautiful marble work to be found in the church. First there is a striking square of inlaid marble, granite and porphyry in the pavement. It did not belong to the original floor but at what point in time it was inserted and what its meaning was is uncertain. Above the imperial door on the inside you will see a marble inlaid panel of an altar with a cross. Around the decorative roundels on the left and the right are depicted dolphins, that continue to swim in the Bosphorus.

The Galleries

The galleries were used as the women's quarters, although in later times they were reserved for the Empress and her retinue. In the course of time a multitude of imperial loges and oratories for private devotion were left here. The galleries were also used for somewhat less edifying practices since the Council in Trullo (692) deemed it necessary to inveigh against those who were having intercourse here.

The northern gallery is the best place to begin. The only thing of interest is the mosaic of Emperor Alexander (912-13). It is hard to find since it is squeezed onto a patch high on the sidewall of the northwest pier that lies immediately to the right. The fact that it has such an obscure place is quite appropriate for this extremely cruel despot whose chief merit was that his reign lasted only thirteen months. When the Emperor died of a stroke during a drunken game of polo, the people knew that this was a clear case of divine retribution. After all Alexander had made pagan sacrifices to the statues in the Hippodrome in order to cure the impotence that he had inflicted upon himself by his debaucheries.

All the decoration in the western gallery was painted by Fossati but some of the original mosaic decoration remains on the gallery level. This part of the gallery was reserved for the Empress. The circle of green marble set into the floor was the site of her throne.

Turning into the south gallery you pass through a marble partition, the bays beyond were set aside for a variety of uses by the clergy and the Emperor. At the east end of the gallery are two interesting mosaics. The first one depicts the infamous Empress Zoë (1028-50) and her third husband Constantine IX Monomachos (1042-55), with the enthroned figure of Christ between them, his right hand raised in the Orthodox gesture of benediction. The Emperor is offering to Christ the traditional *apokombion*, his gift of a purse of gold soldi (the currency of the time). While the complexion of Constantine is rugged and sanguinary, Zoë's face is almost like a doll; the cheeks are highly rouged and the shadows of the brows are intensified in the manner of modern make-up. Here we see the old Empress in persistent pursuit of youth. Luckily enough, the setting-bed of the dilapidated section of the figure of Zoë has survived, allowing us to discern the original fresco, painted in situ by the mosaicist, as a guide to the setting of his cubes.

The second mosaic again depicts an imperial pair, John Comnenus (1118-43) and the pious Empress Irene, daughter of the King of Hungary, with the Mother of God between them. The main panel was set up about 1118, when John came to the throne. In 1122 their own Alexius was proclaimed co-Emperor, and in that year his portrait was added to the left of Irene.

The mosaic with the most recent date is the Deesis mosaic from the thirteenth century. It represents Christ flanked by St. John the Baptist—whom the Byzantines called Prodomos the Forerunner—and the Mother of God. They are pleading with Christ as it was widely believed that all men could be saved by their prayers.

In the floor opposite the Deesis is the tombstone of Enrico Dandolo, the cunning Doge of Venice, who was the mastermind behind the conquest of Constantinople. It therefore comes as no surprise that the people threw his bones to the dogs.

The glass fittings between the stones of the wall are used to check the dome's balance. Many columns also have a pronounced lean, revealing the fact that the church is slowly yielding under the weight of ages. As a consequence continuous restoration is vital, and only the lucky can today see the interior without scaffolding obstructing the view.

Murder in the Imperial Palace

When Constantine VIII died, he ordered his fifty-year-old daughter Zoë, who was still a virgin, to be married to Romanus Argyros (1028-34). It is said that Zoë was almost embarrassingly enthusiastic about the proposal. When the new Empress did not bring forth the much-wanted heir, Romanus refused to share her bed. That was a huge mistake for the Empress was in love with a stable boy and now had other options. Michael Psellus lets us know that she *"could neither regard the young man with philosophic detachment, nor control her desires. The young man supposed that the invitation to visit her was due to her kindness of heart, and he accepted it, although in a modest and timorous fashion. This bashful reserve made him the more dazzling (...) Later his advances became more brazen and she clung to him all the closer. Her kisses became more passionate, she truly loving him, he in no way desiring her (for she was past the age of love), but thinking in his heart of the glory that power would bring him."* Passion led the Empress on to crime. Together they plotted the Emperor's downfall and when the poison that they gave him took too long, Michael decided to drown Romanus in his bath. During the reign of Michael IV (1034-41), he substituted the face of Romanus on the mosaic with his own. When he eventually passed away, his face was replaced with that of his odious nephew who imprisoned Zoë and destroyed both faces in the Hagia Sophia. But as the people held a place in their hearts for the old Empress who was born long before this young upstart, a general uproar followed in the course of which he was blinded. Zoë then married the handsome (!) Constantine Monomachus (1042-55) whose face you see before you now. The only thing we don't know is why the face of Christ was also destroyed. Perhaps the artist, drawing new portraits of Zoë and Constantine, decided to supplant the head of Christ too, in the interest of the unity of his painting.

The Hippodrome

In Constantinople the three centers of power were situated close to each other. First of all there was the Great Palace, the seat of imperial power. Opposite the palace stood the Hagia Sophia, the Vatican of the East, and then there was the Hippodrome, the racecourse and the center of civilian life. So the will of the Emperor, of God, and of the people could all be heard here.

The Hippodrome

The Hippodrome (from the Latin, *dromos*, to run and *hippo*, horse) was originally built by the Roman Emperor Septimus Severus in 203 on the model of the Circus Maximus in Rome. Constantine rebuilt the semi-circular part (known as the sphendone). Because the hill was not long enough to serve as a racetrack, they had to build a huge substructure on which the tiers could be placed. At the top of the outer wall a colonnade circumvented the racetrack in the classical manner. The engraving, seen here, depicts the Hippodrome in the mid-sixteenth century when many columns were still standing. The racetrack was 117.5 meters wide and 480 meters long and could seat up to 40,000 people.

The royal loge (kathisma) was located at the opposite end of the *sphendone*, approximately where the neo-Byzantine fountain of Kaiser Wilhelm now stands. The Emperor, surrounded by his family and favored courtiers, would sit here and watch the daylong games. The imperial lodge was in direct communication with the palace as a safety measure. A little below the imperial box was a platform raised on twenty-four porphyry columns that was reserved for the imperial guard and the orchestra. The columns now adorn the courtyard of the Süleymaniye Mosque. The famous bronze horses of Lysippus that now grace the San Marco Basilica in Venice stood on top of the *kathisma*.

The backbone of the Hippodrome was the *spina*, a podium that divided the racetrack in two and connected a long series of statues, obelisks and columns. On the list of the ancient treasures of the Hippodrome are the she-wolf suckling Romulus and Remus, the incomparable statue of Helen and the mighty Hercules. The list is endless. Bishop Eusebius was shocked when he saw all those heathen statues but he justified his beloved Emperor by saying that Constantine had only erected them here so that they would be the subject of ridicule and contempt by the people.

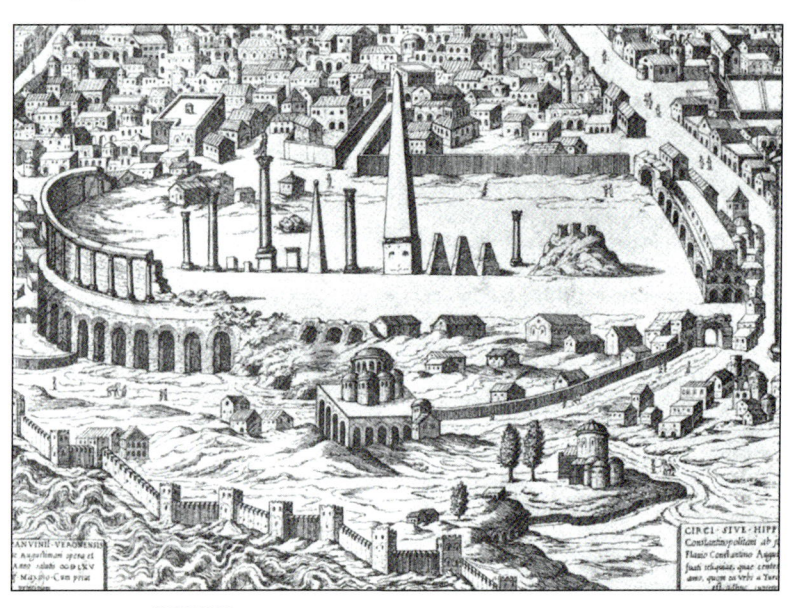

Fights of beasts and gladiators were not held in the Hippodrome. Instead circus-like entertainment was provided between the races; there were dancing bears, tightrope walkers, jugglers, etc. Executions and public punishments also took place here. Disobedient patriarchs were flogged and heretics burned. Since the Hippodrome was the place where the people could voice their concerns, they could present their petitions here.

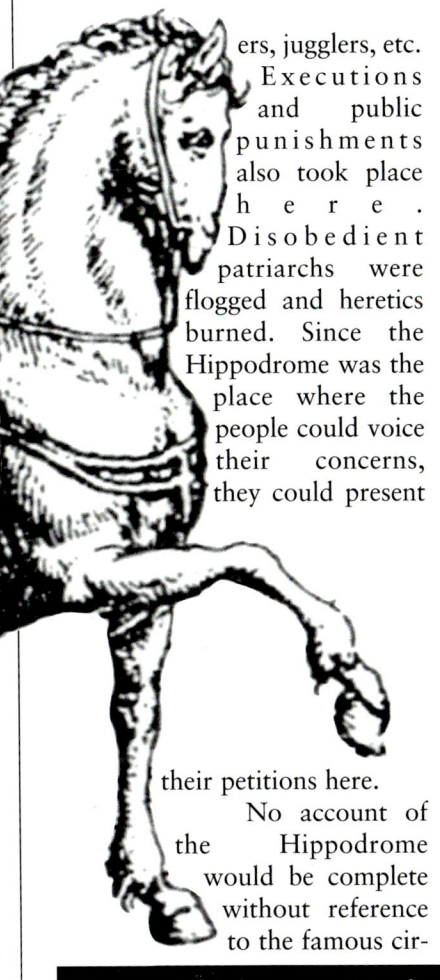

No account of the Hippodrome would be complete without reference to the famous circus factions, the Blues and the Greens. It would not be wrong to think of them as big sporting associations, clubs with a formidable organization, with their own stables, horses, stud farms, with their employees, grooms, jockeys and their subscribing members. Unlike the clubs of today, however, these factions had civilian tasks too. The walls were built with their aid and they had to assist the Emperor in all kinds of state ceremonials. The two factions were normally mortal enemies of each other and that is why the Blues sat on the left of the Emperor and the Greens on the right. At stake was not only the winning of the race but political and theological issues as well. So if the Green party won, everyone wearing the blue badge was dishonored. Insults would be hurled at them in the street and they would angrily wait for the next race to take revenge. The situation is not unlike today's atmosphere at the football matches. A chronicler at the time of Justinian writes, "The horse-races turn the minds more in a state of frenzy then joy and the supporters are ready to commit every conceivable crime for their faction. Regrettably the delirium which bring the races about is a very widespread form of insanity in the Empire."

How a Dishonest Prefect was Brought to Justice

One day, the Prefect of the Palace confiscated a merchant vessel on some slight pretext. The widow, who was the owner of the ship, tried every possible way to be heard, but the sly prefect was able to frustrate all her efforts after justice and prevented the knowledge of his crime from reaching the Emperor. At last the outraged lady asked the pantomimes of the Hippodrome for help. They made a tiny ship which they placed in front of the Emperor's box. One of the clowns called to another, "Here, big mouth, swallow that ship." "My mouth is not big enough to swallow it," was the reply. "What, you cannot swallow that little ship?" said the other clown astonished. "The Prefect has just swallowed a big galley with cargo and he did not even leave one bite to the owner." Of course the Emperor wanted to know what was going on and since the trembling prefect had no good excuse, he was immediately put to death in the Hippodrome, still wearing his gala robes of office.

The Nika Rebellion

The famous Nika rebellion started on January 13, 532. Part of the palace was destroyed and the original Hagia Sophia burned down. Justinian went to the Hippodrome to make apologies but he was stoned and instead the people raised an unwilling nephew of Justinian to the purple. After five days of great turmoil the scared generals advised the Emperor to flee. But then Empress Theodora entered the council chamber delivering this memorable speech:

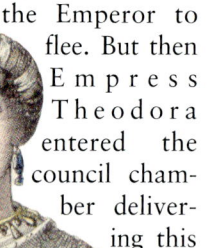

"Death is the condition of our birth; but they who have reigned should never survive the loss of dignity and dominion. I implore heaven, that I may never be seen, not a day, without my diadem and purple; that I may no longer behold the light, when I cease to be saluted with the name of queen. If you resolve, O Caesar! to fly, you have treasures; behold the sea, you have ships; but tremble lest the desire of life should expose you to wretched exile and ignominious death. For my own part, I adhere to the maxim of antiquity, that the throne is glorious sepulchre."

This formidable talk restored the courage of the court and the generals decided to launch an all-out attack with their crack troops. They burst open the two opposite gates of the Hippodrome and marched in, sword in hand, taking no prisoners. Thirty thousand were slain that day and their blood colored the statues red. Justinian's nephew was found and executed on the spot since, as Gibbon so aptly states, his crime was manifest and his innocence uncertain. The partisans were buried where they fell and since that time one of the entrances of the Hippodrome has been called the Nekra Porta, the Gate of Death.

Until the time of Justinian, games were a constant occurrence. As time went on they became less frequent, and were in the end celebrated only twice a year, on December 25, marking the birth of Christ and on May 11, the anniversary of the founding of the city. The decline of the races was not only a question of money but also of mentality. The classical city could not do without the games, in medieval times it became more a tradition to be upheld than anything else. After the conquest of Constantinople by the Latins the races ceased and in Ottoman times, the Hippodrome became known as the At Meydanı (the Square of Horses), and games of javelin were played there.

The Present-Day Monuments

The Egyptian Obelisk

The porphyry obelisk of Theodosius is the best preserved of the three monuments that remain standing on the Hippodrome. This monolith originally stood in the vicinity of Thebes and commemorated "a great massacre" for which Pharaoh Thutmose (1490-1436 BC) was responsible when he defeated the Syrians. The obelisk was erected during the reign of Theodosius I (379-95), the first Emperor to make Christianity the state religion. The obelisk confesses his defeat in an inscription at the marble basis:

"Difficult was once the command to obey serene sovereigns and to yield the victory to dead kings. But to Theodosius and his perennial offspring all things submit. So I, too, was conquered, and in thirty days under Proclus the prefect I was raised to the upper air."

The Greek inscription tells us that thirty-two days were needed, so one wonders if the stonemasons were not on speaking terms. The fact that the inscription is bilingual attests that the native tongue, Greek, was already regarded as equal in importance to the official tongue brought by the Romans.

On the marble base we see the Emperor and his family seated in the imperial box. The stiffness of the attitudes reflects a new style that was not interested in the naturalistic depiction of the human form and valued expressiveness more then delicacy.

On the northern face, where there is a drainage channel, the Emperor is depicted watching the erection of the obelisk; further down the monolith is shown lying on the ground with cords and capstans being worked by slaves. The Chi-Ro monogram that alludes to the first letters of the Savior (X=*Chi* and P = *ro*, so *Chri-stos*) is carved above the drainage channel. When an angel appeared to him in a dream ordering him to do so, Constantine put this sign on the shields of his soldiers to ensure his victory. On the western face is the Emperor receiving homage from vanquished enemies. On the southern face the Emperor watches the races depicted in the lower block. Finally on the eastern side, the Emperor is handing garlands to the winners in the midst of singers and dancers while an orchestra plays double Lydian flutes and pipes.

Other Monuments

The Serpent Column commemorated the Greek victory over the Persians in the battle of Plataea (479 BC). The column stood in or outside the temple of Apollo in Delphi and was made out of the shields of the conquered Persian soldiers. On some coils there are some faint traces left of the names of thirty-two Greek cities that had been engraved on the column. The heads are lost but the upper jaw of one of the serpent's heads can be seen in the Archeological Museum.

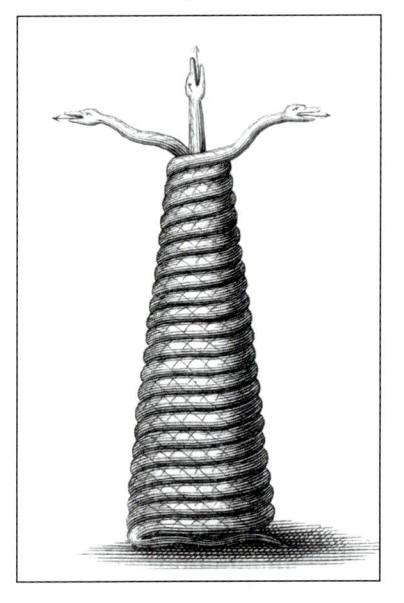

The last monument is the roughly built stone obelisk, called the Column of Constantine Porphyrogenitus, after Emperor Constantine (912-59), who restored this monument of the fourth century. He had it encased in bronze gilt, but greedy crusaders stripped the bronze so that only the gaping holes left by the bolts and nails which held the plates in place can now be seen. The inscription boasts that, *"the Colossus of Rhodos was a marvel there, so is this Colossus of Constantine a marvel here."* Today it is really hard to appreciate this melancholic pile of stones.

An Enjoyable Stroll

From the top of the *sphendone*, the semi-circular end of the Hippodrome, there is an outstanding view of the city and the Marmara Sea. At your right in the distance are the land walls; in the foreground, just behind the railway line stands the Church of SS. Sergius and Bacchus (see the District of the Great Palace) which is now used as a mosque. The green area with lots of trees is the Kadırga Square of which we will come to speak in the next chapter.

Keep walking downhill, following the bends in the street, to the great supporting wall of the sphendone. Its arches were bricked up in later time to prevent the collapse of the structure.

The District of the Great Palace

The fabled Great Palace of the Byzantine emperors roughly stood where the Blue Mosque now stands. From there it stretched out to the sea, virtually occupying the whole area that is now called Cankurtaran. With its quaint wooden houses, Cankurtaran is still one of the most pleasant neighborhoods of the city. If you wander around, you will find bits and pieces of old Byzantium everywhere you go.

The Mosaic Museum

We tend to think of a palace as one single building, but the Great Palace consisted of courtyards, gardens, streets, audience halls, manufacturers, stables, chapels, churches and pavilions. In short it was a little city in itself, as was later the Seraglio of the Ottoman sultans. Today virtually nothing of this vast complex of buildings stands above the ground.

The most magnificent remaining part of the palace is the mosaic pavement of the Chrysotriclinium, the throne room. Fifty years ago British archeologists dug up a large *peristylar* court and an aligning palace meeting hall. The Imperial Palace can at best be imagined as a grand playhouse where an intricate court ceremonial was enacted. The Emperor did not change his clothes, but dressed himself liked an actor and it was said that while others just came in, he appeared. Many of the rooms of the palace were for this reason more stagedecors than anything else.

The walls of the palace were adorned with silk hangings and rare marbles, with Persian carpets covering the floor. *"Everything was so rich here,"* reported one of the astonished Crusaders *"that there was not a hinge nor a band nor any other part such as is usually made of iron that was not all of silver, and there was no column that was not of porphyry or some rich precious stone."* The mosaic floor gives us an idea of the sheer sumptuousness lavished on the palace. Since only the best was good enough for the emperors, we now have the opportunity to admire the largest and most beautiful mosaic pavement of the classical world.

The colonnaded hall in which we see the mosaic pavement was, in layout and decoration, not much different from the palaces of ancient Rome and was in the past ascribed to the time of Constantine. However, recent research has unquestionably proven that the construction work took place under the reign of the great Justinian, when the palace was enlarged and renovated. The craftsmen used a wide variety of colors for the floor: glass cubes in red, blue, green and black, brick cubes (terracotta) and occasionally some semiprecious stones. In 1982 the Austrian Academy of Science restored the mosaics, which were in a state of total decay.

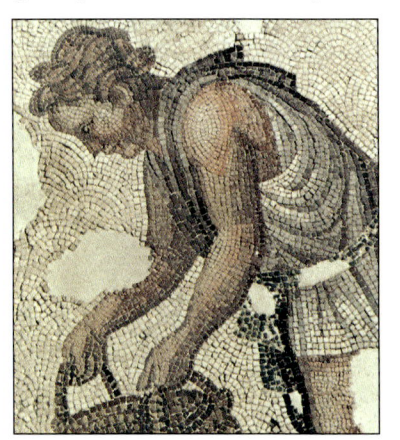

Although the floor was made by Christian artists, there is nothing evidently Christian about it. The subject of the mosaics is an idealized version of rural life, as opposed to the decadent ways of the city. Apart from country scenes there are also mythological compositions, such as the Bellerophon and the Chimera. The frame with its acanthus scroll alludes to the world of Dionysus, god of life's energy. There are exotic fruits, populated with a host of animals. Even the tiny grasshopper, hiding among the leaves, has not been left out. Occasionally scenes do carry a meaning. The four boys with hoops imitate the races at the Hippodrome. The two turning columns indicate the racecourse. The fight between an eagle and a snake symbolizes the Emperor's victory over his enemies.

The Magnaura, the Bucoleon and the Sea Walls

Until very recently nothing was thought to have survived from the palace, which the Greeks called the Palace of the Fresh Breeze. Construction work in the area and the completion of the posh Four Seasons Hotel, however, have uncovered the Magnaura which is now being somewhat insensitively rebuilt. Only the underground structures of the Magnaura are to be seen and it may not be much, but the masonry is impressive and all the time you feel as if you could stumble over hidden treasures. It was in this palace that Bishop Liutprand of Cremona, the German ambassador, was invited. His description of the audience gives us further insight into the ostentatious court ritual.

"As the Emperor approached, the choir began to cry out in adulation; 'Behold the morning star approaches, in his eyes the sun's rays are reflected, Nicephorus our prince, the pale death of the Saracens' (...) before the Emperor's throne stood a tree, made of bronze, whose branches were filled with birds, also made of gilded bronze, which uttered different cries. Now the Emperor's throne was made in such a cunning manner that at one moment it was down on the ground, while at another it rose higher and was seen to be up in the air. This throne was of immense size and was guarded by bronze lions, covered with gold, beating the ground with their tails and roared with open mouth and quivering tongue."

The Imperial Palace was a house of marvels, with all kinds of mechanical inventions, called automata, to impress the visiting dignitaries. However the Great Palace was not only a place for show but also for learning. While in the West the classical heritage of the sciences became the preserve of the clergy, in Byzantium secular learning continued to flourish and an important philosophy and law faculty was located in the Magnaura Palace.

At the very opposite extremity of the palace was another distinct complex, known as the Bucoleon. Its name was derived from a marble group of a Lion and a Bull standing upon the harbor's quay in front of the palace. Stone lions belonging to this palace now adorn a staircase in the Archeological Museum. If you take the main road that leads down to the sea and turn left, you will be a few minutes away from a ruined but still beautiful tenth century façade with marble framed windows. On the left of the façade is a ruined marble staircase. Cars now come roaring past but until the beginning of the sixties when the coast road was constructed, the sea came up to the palace.

Perhaps you have heard the name Porpyrogenitus before. This title had no official authority since you could be a great emperor without being "Porphyrogenitus," but to be able to say that you were was a very prestigious affair because it designated someone who was born in the purple room of the palace. Anna Comnena, the favorite daughter of Emperor Alexius describes this famous room:

"It looks out on to the sea and the harbor (...) the floor and the walls are covered in marble ñ not the common sort, nor even the kind that is costly but obtainable, but that which the earlier Emperors had carried of from Rome. This marble is, roughly speaking, purple, but it has small dots like white sand sprinkled all over it. I think, that our ancestors called the chamber therefore 'purple.'"

The sections of the walls facing the Marmara Sea that can still be seen today date from the ninth century. These walls were significantly damaged when the railroad lines were laid in 1871-72. The fortifications extended from the Seraglio point to the southern extremity of the land walls, near Yedikule, and consisted of a single wall flanked by 188 towers, a total length of some eight kilometers. Special sea gates allowed ships to enter since the shoreline was dotted with harbors. The neighborhood around the Church of Sergius and Bacchus is, for example, called Kadırga, which means "galley," and is a reminder of the harbor that still existed in early Ottoman times.

These walls stood close to the water's edge, making it virtually impossible to land troops at their feet. The biggest danger therefore came from the sea. That is why the line of the wall's course was extremely irregular, turning in and out with every bend of the shore, to present as short and sharp a front as possible to the angry waves that dashed against them.

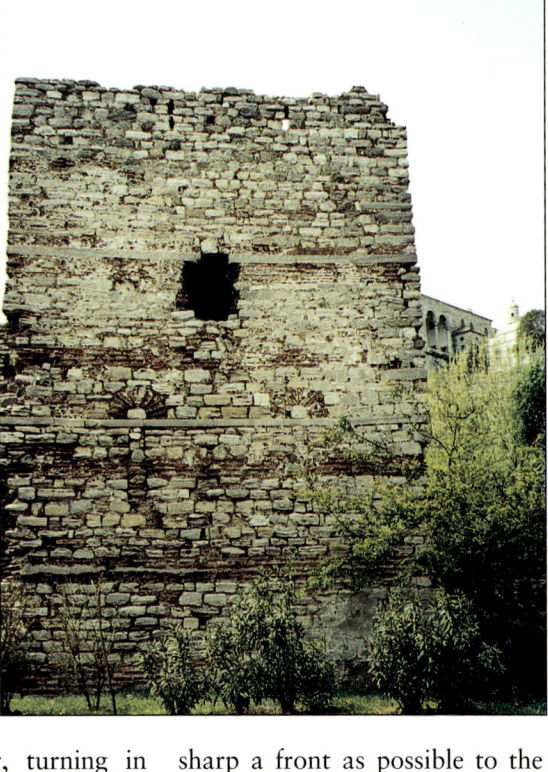

To the attentive eye there is much to discover. There is, for instance, a little gate with posts made of marble lintels, carved with verses in Greek taken from the book Habakkuk and the Psalms. Some people suggest that it once formed the base of an equestrian statue of Justinian. The fact that the Byzantines used what must have been a venerable monument as building material tells us something about the sad state of the Empire during its last days.

Küçük Ayasofya

A little bit further on is an ancient building behind the walls. The small church dedicated to Saints Sergius and Bacchus is one of the most charming of all Byzantine churches in the city. In 1503 the church was converted into a mosque and ever since that day people speak of Küçük (little) Aya Sofya.

Sergius and Bacchus were two Roman soldiers who were persecuted because of their beliefs and died as martyrs. Under Constantine they became the patron saints of the army. When Justinian was under sentence of death, having been accused of plotting against his uncle the Emperor, two saints appeared in a dream to Anastatius pleading with him not to kill his nephew. No one can accuse Justinian of being ungrateful, because when he came to the throne in 527, he built this sweet little church in their memory.

The Church of Saints Sergius and Bacchus is an architecturally striking building. The plan is a square with a dome. Columned *exedras* fill out the angles of the square under the domed vaults, and the piers supporting the dome form an octagon. The number eight is perhaps not randomly chosen since it might allude to eternity. In the mystical universe of the devout Byzantine, everything carried meaning. Sunday was called the eighth day. After the week, which stood for our migratory existence, there was Sunday, the day on which the church celebrated the resurrection of Christ and the gift of eternal life.

Unfortunately all the mosaic decoration and marbles adorning the walls have disappeared and the building is in a sad state of repair. Curiously enough the mosque's courtyard has been fully restored while the ancient structure, mentioned in all art history books, is on the verge of collapse.

This church heralds, in style and decoration, the beginning of a new age, where an abstract idea in the mind has come to count for more than the celebration of the natural world. The lace-like capitals replacing the Corinthian capitals, with their fidelity to nature, are good examples of this development.

In the midst of architrave and cornice runs a Greek inscription, which reads:

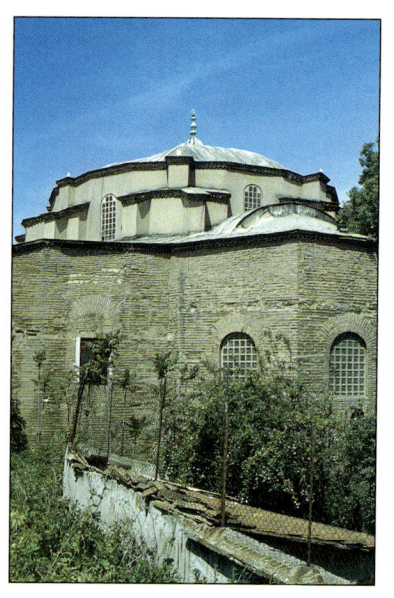

"Other Emperors have honoured dead heroes whose achievement was small: but our sceptre-bearing Justinian, inspired by piety, glorifies with a magnificent church Sergius, the servant of the Omnipotent Christ; him neither the kindling breath of fire, nor the sword, nor any other sort of torture shook: for the divine Christ he endured, and, though slain, he gained the kingdom of heaven by his blood. Forever may he hold in his keeping the reign of the vigilant Emperor, and augment the power of Theodora, he divinely crowned; of her, whose mind is filled with piety, and whose labour and constant exertions are directed to the diffusion of temporal blessings."

Nearby is the lovely square of Kadırga, the area of one of the ancient ports of Byzantium.

Hagia Eirene and the Palace Gardens

The former gardens of the Topkapı Palace are a good place to recover from the hustle and bustle of the city. Our starting point for this pleasant stroll of not more than an hour, is the Hagia Eirene, one of the biggest and oldest Byzantine churches in the city. After that, we will take a leisurely stroll through the gardens to one of the nicest tea terraces of the city.

Hagia Eirene

The Hagia Eirene, a major Byzantine church, is located in the first courtyard of the Topkapı Palace. This church was erected here in 532 following the famous Nika riots that had destroyed a great part of the city. In the time of Constantine there was already a church in this place and excavations have revealed the remains of an Aphrodite temple on which St. Irene is partly built. The Hagia Eirene, the Church of Divine Wisdom and the Church of Divine Peace, were essentially two parts of one large religious complex, connected to each other by porticos. This church was never converted into a mosque because it was used as an arsenal in the defense of the palace. The presently empty building serves occasionally as a concert and exhibition hall, although unfortunately it is usually closed.

The church, a basilica with a cupola, is almost devoid of decoration. The only "real" mosaic to be seen is that of a large cross in the apse. The apse itself is interesting because it still has a *synthronon*, a Greek name for the benches on which the priests sat during service. A few capitals still bear the monograms of Justinian and Theodora.

The remains of the Hospice of Samson lie behind the church. It is often suggested that the Byzantines had a superb healthcare system. Constantinople had hospitals, poorhouses, homes for the blind and the aged, homes for repentant prostitutes, maternity wards, psychiatric clinics and orphanages, and everything was free of charge. Despite the fact that even great scholars have romanticized this aspect of the Byzantine past, reality is more sobering. For example, John Comnenus, nicknamed the Good (depicted in the Hagia Sophia) built a (large!) charitable foundation at the Pantocrator Church, including a home for the elderly. So far everything sounds commendable, but the hospital only had 50 beds (only 12 for women!), while the elderly home had room for 24 persons. Supposing there were 100 hospitals and other institutions, then 2400 persons could receive care, out of a population that ranked most likely above the figure of 250,000. Even if this number is doubled, it is obvious that only the happy few of the destitute and the poor could get some help. The vast majority must have lived in unbelievable squalor, to which every third world country today would pale in comparison. Constantinople was no doubt a little shop of horrors.

Gülhane Park

There is no need to retrace your steps because a little alley leads down to the recently restored Darphane, the buildings of the Ottoman Mint which are now exhibition halls. A little bit farther downhill is the Archeological Museum.

Although the main part of the museum is devoted to the Ancient East and the Roman Age Empire, there is a very pretty section at the back of the main building solely devoted to Byzantium. There are mosaic floors, icons, a pedestal from the Hippodrome, jewels and utensils. Particularly interesting are a number of Byzantine sculptures because they are much rarer than icons and the like. When the weather is nice, you can sit in the outdoor cafe under the trees surrounded by broken bits and pieces of old Byzantium.

After passing the museum, you will come to Gülhane Park, which was part of the Topkapı Palace gardens until the nineteenth century.

To the rear of the park is the Goth's column. This granite column belonged to the *spina* of a Roman theater and is perhaps the only monument still standing dating from before the founding of Constantinople. The inscription on the base reads, *"Fortuna reduci ob devictos Gothes,"* and probably refers to the victory over the Goths in 259 AD by Claudius II. We are not sure however if it was erected at that time or later in Constantine's days. Sources tell us that the column was once topped by a statue of Byzans, the legendary founder of Byzantium.

There are several nice teahouses built on terraces in this area. From them Üsküdar and Kadıköy are visible on the opposite shore. It was here that the blind from the legend founded their city. Üsküdar was anciently known as Chrysopolis, the City of Gold but in spite of its name it was—as is the case today—just a suburb of more fashionable Kadıköy, or Chalcedon. In church history this place is important because it was here that the Fourth Ecumenical Council was held in 451.

Detail of the Jeruselem Mosaic, Archeological Museum

Theological Debates in the City

There were several heresies that threatened to divide the church and the councils that intended to formulate the right path. The Orthodox point of view is that Christ must be fully God and fully man; fully God, because it is clear that only a god can save us. But only if Christ is truly man, as we are, can we participate in what He had done for us. God became man that we might be made God said St. Athanasios. The Greek fathers always liked to put an emphasis on the fact that man could become God and in this respect they placed a far greater confidence in man's divine inheritance than the great church father of the West, St. Augustine, who tainted man's nature with original sin.

Nonetheless, each heresy tried to undermine some part of the creed. Arius made Christ a second-rate God; Nestorius divided the manhood in Christ from his Godhead and turned Christ more or less into a mere inspired mortal, and finally the monk Eutyches denied the human nature of Christ, using the mystical image that the human nature of Christ had disappeared like a moth in the flame. This monophysitic view that Christ had only one single nature was condemned at the Council of Chalcedon, for they wanted to emphasize that God had truly suffered and was not simply a phantom, who was above that.

The theological issues at stake may have been comparatively small but the political consequences were enormous because they undermined state security. The Nestorians were welcomed by the Persian monarch, and by the seventh century the monophysite churches had seceded, and the bulk of their flocks had converted to Islam.

Although these religious controversies may seem far-fetched today, they were not for the average Byzantine. Theological dispute was never the preserve of the clergy. There is a funny and appropriate passage in the work of St. Gregory of Nyssa (fourth century), which illustrates this:

"Constantinople is full of tradesmen and slaves who are all of them profound theologians, and preach in shops and in the streets. When I ask how many coppers I must pay, he informs me wherein the Son differs from the Father; if you ask the price of bread, you are told that the Son is inferior to the Father; and if I ask my servant if my bath is ready, he replies that Son was created from nothing."

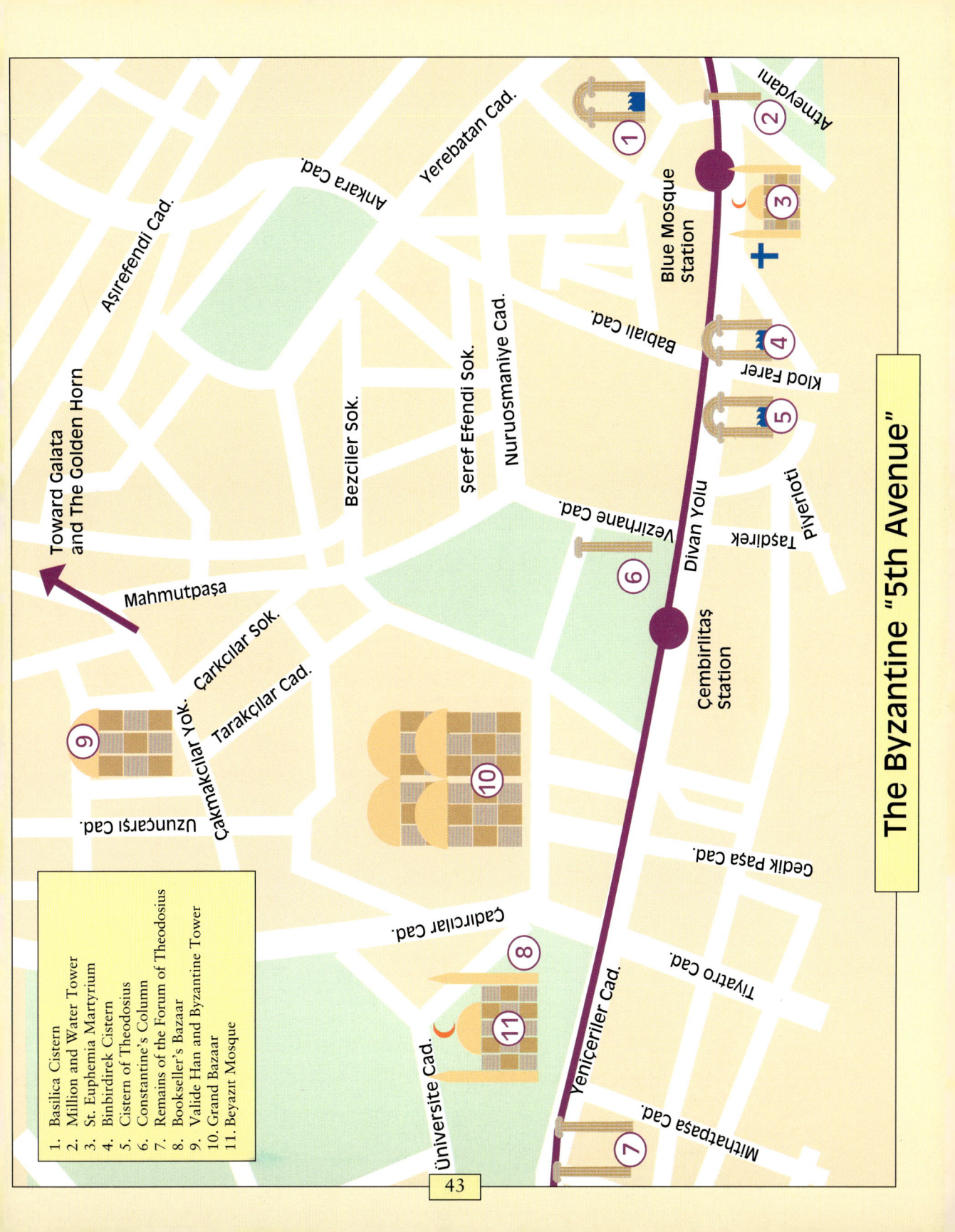

The Byzantine "5th Avenue"

1. Basilica Cistern
2. Million and Water Tower
3. St. Euphemia Martyrium
4. Binbirdirek Cistern
5. Cistern of Theodosius
6. Constantine's Column
7. Remains of the Forum of Theodosius
8. Bookseller's Bazaar
9. Valide Han and Byzantine Tower
10. Grand Bazaar
11. Beyazıt Mosque

43

The Byzantine 5th Avenue

While walking along the main thoroughfare of Byzantine times, I will tell you a bit more about how the city looked in antiquity and show you the way to a long forgotten Byzantine tower, from which you will have one of the finest views in the city

The Mese and Augustaeum

The Mese, or Central Street, was the main thoroughfare leading to the heart of the city, starting across from the Hagia Sophia. It was the smartest shopping district of the city. The modern Divan Yolu and Yeniçeriler Caddesi still follow the course of the Mese. Along this wide street with arcades on either side were the most expensive shops, arranged in groups according to their wares - the gold and silversmiths, the clothiers, the furniture-makers and so on. This shows how the idea of grouping various trades together goes back to Byzantine times. Officials inspected shops, checked weights and measures and the quality of the merchandise. The export of luxury goods was strictly controlled, since their rarity and price had to be maintained. The Byzantine economy was totally regulated by the state and everything was circumscribed. Money could only be lent at a fixed rate of interest, and all products had a fixed price, the hours of labor were also strictly specified.

In front of the Hagia Sophia lay a great square, which Constantine had named Augustaeum in memory of his mother, Helena Augusta. On one side stood the famous public baths of Zeuxippos, on the other the palace of the Patriarch. The chief entrance to the Great Palace was also located here. It was called the Chalke or Bronze House and had a great mosaic of Christ above the doors. In the middle of the square stood an equestrian statue of Justinian who was vain enough to have himself depicted as the agile Achilles. One extremely pitiful piece of stone belonging to the Augustaeum still remains. At the corner of the entrance to the Yerebatan Cistern stands a marble column belonging to the Million, the starting-point from which the distances were reckoned over the Empire. Next to it stands another Byzantine structure, which was perhaps used as a water tower to keep the pressure of the water up.

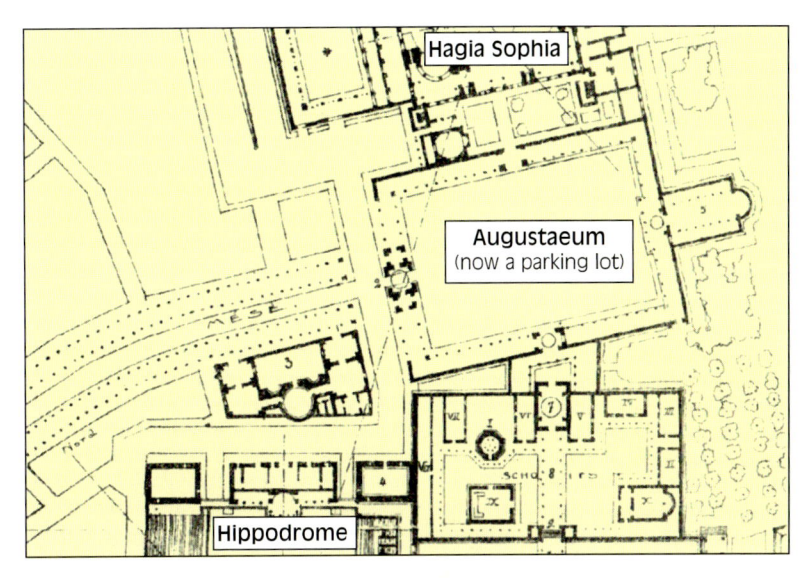

What kind of people would you have seen walking on the streets in ancient times? Although it has been said that the Byzantine Empire based itself on Greek learning and language, this doesn't mean that the inhabitants of the city were pure Greeks. Like the American population today, the Byzantine population was the product of a great melting pot of many different cultures and the proportion of pure Greeks was probably very small. Constantinople was a cosmopolitan city and consequently there was no racial prejudice among the Byzantines even though the Byzantines felt a deep contempt for foreigners. The nobles were very discontented when Justinian II forced a senator to marry his Negro cook, but that was more a matter of snobbery than racial dislike. Everyone who borrowed the Byzantine trappings and was Orthodox (or at least behaved like it) was most welcome.

Along the Divan Yolu

Start walking down the Divan Yolu. To the left behind the austere Firuz Ağa Mosque lies the scanty remains of a martyrium (seventh century) for St. Euphemia. Her body lies buried in the Patriarchal Church in Fener.

Further down the avenue is the (new) entrance to the Binbirdirek Cistern (see next chapter). A little bit further lies the Pierre Loti Hotel and, in the side street next to it, the cistern of Theodosius.

By now you will have noticed a large pillar in the distance. It is the porphyry column of Constantine, erected by him to commemorate the dedication of the city as the capital of the Roman Empire (May 11, 330). The column was crowned by a statue of the Emperor in the form of a radiant Apollo. That Constantine, although Christian, found no difficulty in posing as the Sun God, reveals that he might not have lost all of his heathen sympathies. It is said that in order to honor his pagan and Christian citizens, Constantine buried several relics under the column, like the Palladium of Troy (a sacred wooden figure of Athena), the axe of Noah and the remains of the seven loaves (!). The ungainly base was added at the end of the seventeenth century after a great fire weakened the structure. At that time the iron bans around it were renewed, and that is why today the Turks speak of Çemberlitaş, the hooped column. Most guidebooks speak of the burned column. The column stood in the middle of the Forum of Constantine.

The road leads on to the Great Bazaar and the early sixteenth century Beyazıt Mosque. A bit further on, you will see the pillars and decorated lintels of a Roman triumphal arch. These are the only remains of the Forum Tauri or Forum Theodosius. From this public space two principal arteries branched off. One led to the church of the Holy Apostles (on the spot of the Fatih Mosque) and then to the Edirne Gate, the other one passed through the Golden Gate.

The Sahaflar Çarşısı, or Booksellers' Bazaar, wedged between the Grand Bazaar and the Beyazıt Mosque is one of the most ancient markets in the city. In Byzantine days, people also sold and bought books here. It is worth walking from here to a Byzantine tower. If you leave the Booksellers' Bazaar behind, you will pass a big plane tree (also called the Tree of Idleness). Here you may ask directions to the Valide Han. This will take you through the heart of the commercial district. The seventeenth century Valide Han is an Ottoman trade building. Once in the big courtyard, you can climb the stairs and ask to go onto the roof. The workers here will know what you want and will unlock the door for you. From the roof you will see a ruined Byzantine tower, which is more or less just the pretext I need to let you enjoy this breathtaking view over this marvelous city I love so much. After admiring the view you can retrace your steps and walk further down the street from which you came. The pretty stone houses here look very Byzantine although they are Ottoman. In ten minutes you will find yourself standing on the shores of the Golden Horn.

The Cisterns of the City

Water supply has up to this very day been a constant concern for the municipality. During Byzantine times, underground water reservoirs were built in all periods. Many of these magnificent structures can still be found, hidden under Istanbul streets and houses.

Constantinople's Cisterns

Constantinople had few water supplies, so the Byzantines had to bring water by aqueducts into their capital, carrying it 25 kilometers from the Belgrade Forest. There are both open and covered cisterns and although it is stated many times that they were built for different purposes, it is not at all clear what the differences were. The most heard theory is that the water in the large open basins was purified by exposure to the air so in the course of time the organic or mineral matter in suspension could settle. There are some questions to be raised here. Would algae and other water flora pollute the water after some time? Although it is tempting to make a comparison with today's water purification basins, it has to be remembered that the Byzantine basins were much bigger and this, according to the experts, makes them unsuitable for their alleged purpose. So what was their use? Perhaps they were just water storage tanks from which the fields were irrigated during dry times. We know that when the big dams were build in the Belgrade Forest in later Byzantine times, the open cisterns fell into disuse and became kitchen gardens. This implies that if the Byzantines could do without them, the open cisterns might not have been used for water purification in the first place.

In any case, when the water arrived in the city, it was led onwards by tunnels big enough to walk in. The older people in Istanbul love to tell stories of a secret maze of underground ways leading from the walls to the Hagia Sophia. Although one might think that this is all pure fantasy, it is not. Near the Hagia Sophia there actually was a water distribution center, so it is likely that many water tunnels lead to this point. All these tunnels had air ventilation shafts. It is said that housewives, believing them wells, used them in summer as refrigerators but when they came back their foodstuffs had all of a sudden mysteriously evaporated, having been taken by the people who were cleaning the tunnels.

The covered cisterns provided drinking water during dry summers. According to Procopius the basilica cistern was especially built for this purpose. This cistern had outgoing pipes by which the tanks and the gardens of the imperial palace were fed. To keep the water reservoirs watertight the builders lined them up to the roof with a special mortar called *koraşan*, consisting of lime, broken brick and tow cut very finely: after eight days this mortar was covered with a coating called *lukium*, composed of slaked lime, linseed oil and cotton waste. There are roughly forty known cisterns in the city but there must be many more. Every once in a while new ones are discovered but only a few are easily accessible.

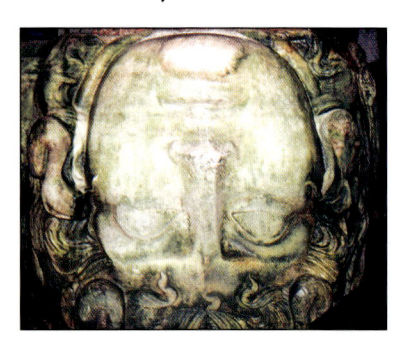

The Basilica Cistern

*S*ize did matter for the great Justinian so it comes as no surprise that the largest and grandest of all the cisterns of Constantinople was erected during his reign. The cistern took his name from the law school basilica, which stood above. The Turks very appropriately call it the Sunken Palace (Yerebatan Saray). The cistern is 140 by 70 meters and there are 336 columns. The wall closing off 90 columns was only built at the end of nineteenth century to fortify the structure. Eight columns have been covered with concrete for the same reason.

Twenty years ago the cistern was totally restored so it is now possible to walk in. Up to that time people could only peek in from the entrance and since its dimensions were not known, it was a source of wild tales. People who ventured into it disappeared and were never seen again while others came back horror-stricken. The cistern provided a wonderful backdrop for the Bond movie *From Russia with Love*. In that film we see 007 crossing the cistern by boat in order to use the telescope that looks into the Russian Consulate.

Corinthian capitals taken from other antique buildings top many columns. The reason that so little of antiquity remains in the city is due to the fact that older buildings were constantly being "recycled." Other capitals were specially cut for the cistern. The most striking leftovers from an ancient building are two gigantic Medusa heads found when 50,000 tons of mud were removed during the restoration. People are fond of tales and that is why they concluded that the heads are upside down so that the evil eye cannot cast its spell. The simpler explanation is that they used the bottom side because it was bigger and thus more suitable to place a column on.

The Binbirdirek Cistern

Rarely visited is the nearby and architecturally interesting cistern of the thousand and one columns (*bin*=1000, *bir*=one, *direk*=column). This cistern is to be transformed into a shopping mall, a questionable idea, but at least the building will be saved from total ruin.

In this cistern two columns are always put on top of each other, hence the name. Actually there are not 1001 columns but 224 to be exact. Their total height is 12.4 meters, and in the middle of the cistern a few of the columns have been dug out. Gazing down one gets a better feel for what an immense work it must have been to remove the mud from the much larger Basilica Cistern. On the capitals are many different stonemason signs but no one knows what their exact use was. Here all of the columns were especially cut for the cistern. This cistern is another masterpiece from the time of Justinian.

Other Cisterns in the City

Under the present Eminönü Belediyesi (City Hall), not far from the Binbirdirek cistern lies the Theodosius cistern. There is even a shield outside that says Theodosius Sarnıç, although it is not a tourist attraction yet. This cistern dates to the fourth century and is one of the oldest in the city. The stairway is closed to visitors but the view from above is very impressive. A peculiarity of this cistern is that it has windows (now walled in) which means that the building must have been standing above the ground and was not dug out like the basilica cistern.

If you want to get the total cistern experience, you can dine in one. The Turkish Touring Club has lovingly restored a small cistern behind the Hagia Sophia in the street of the Cold Fountain (Soğuk Çeşme Sokak). They turned the previous auto-repair workshop into an interesting but rather expensive restaurant decorated in medieval style. Opposite the restaurant there is another small cistern, which is used today as a bar.

There is one more cistern in the vicinity. Halfway into the Gülhane Park is a sign pointing to a rather pitiful aquarium housed in a small cistern, probably dating back to the time of Constantine the Great, making this the oldest cistern in the city.

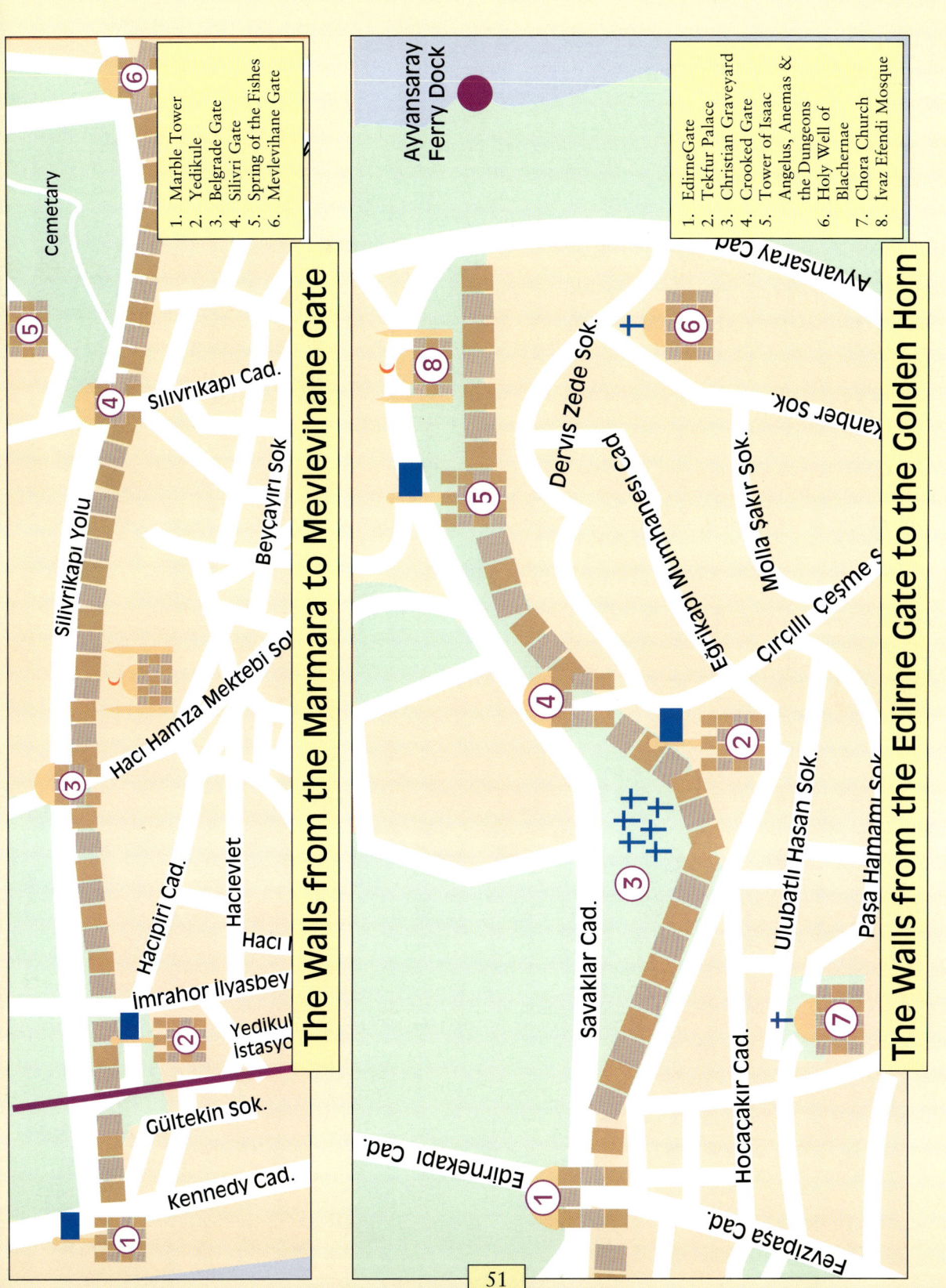

The Land Walls

The Walls from the Marmara to Mevlevihane Gate

1. Marble Tower
2. Yedikule
3. Belgrade Gate
4. Silivri Gate
5. Spring of the Fishes
6. Mevlevihane Gate

The Walls from the Edirne Gate to the Golden Horn

1. Edirne Gate
2. Tekfur Palace
3. Christian Graveyard
4. Crooked Gate
5. Tower of Isaac Angelus, Anemas & the Dungeons
6. Holy Well of Blachernae
7. Chora Church
8. Ivaz Efendi Mosque

The Land Walls

The land walls at the edge of the old city are often seen as simply heaps of old stones. Tourists consequently hardly ever visit them. This is a pity because these impressive walls are as important as the Hagia Sophia. Of course nothing is as neat and clean here as in a museum, but that, in itself, is the charm of these walls. The nineteenth-century travelers understood that very well and they raved about the walls of ancient Constantinople. Edmondo Amici wrote in his famous book on the city:

"Far from oppressing me with any feeling of melancholy, I was conscious of a sensation of exhilaration and excitement: the brilliant vegetation, the cyclopean dimensions of the walls, the great rolling surface of the earth like waves of a mighty ocean, the crowding memories of emperors and armies, of fierce warfare, dead and gone generations, whole nations that had passed away, all flooded my soul and bore me out of myself on a rushing tide of unutterable desires and longings."

Most likely you will not get that carried away with the walls, but it is still easy to get very excited about some sections of this ancient bulwark.

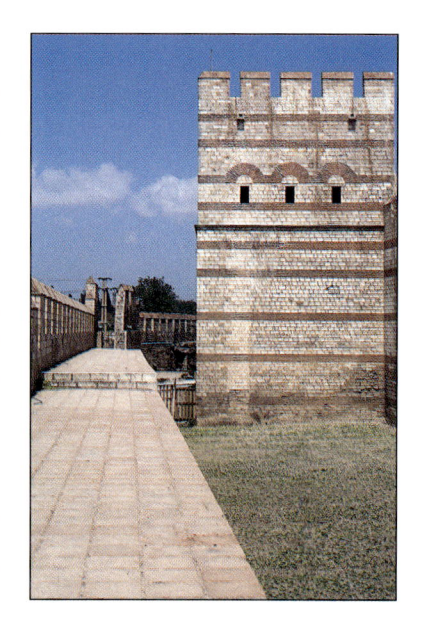

History

As the city of Constantine had rapidly grown beyond her walls, Theodosius II decided in 403 to construct a new wall several kilometers from the old one. The new bulwark consisted initially of a single wall studded with no less then 95 defense towers and it stretched from the Sea of Marmara to the Golden Horn, a distance of 6.5 kilometers. Today the Theodosian wall ends at the Tekfur Palace where the wall of Manuel Comnenos starts, a twelfth century portion of the defense system that we will discuss later. It is said that the factions of the Hippodrome supplied 16,000 men to build the enceinte. In 447 the greater part of the walls was destroyed by a series of violent earthquakes. The disaster was particularly inopportune since Attila the Hun threatened the capital. Constantine, the praetorian prefect, then had the wall rebuilt in less than three months and even managed to improve it. He added an outer wall with a deep moat in front of it, making Constantinople an impregnable bastion for more than a thousand years to come.

The walls were constructed in a typical Byzantine fashion from limestone blocks with bands of brick. Catapults and machines that hurled missiles with Greek fire were placed on the tops of the walls, while sentinels watched the horizon day and night, keeping themselves awake at night by shouting to one another along the line.

The chief function of the terrace between the outer wall and the moat was to widen the distance between the besiegers and the besieged. The moat is divided by partitions at regular intervals; these had a sharp edge at the top to prevent their use by the enemy. Some people say that their function was to prevent communication along the inside of the moat, but that does not explain why there are buttresses built against these partitions. This gives support to the idea that they were built to strengthen the partitions when they were flooded. Partitions were needed to hold the water because of the irregular slope of the ground. Whether or not the moat was filled with water is still a topic of debate. We do know for sure that the moat was not flooded during the last siege of 1453. Perhaps the moat was flooded in peacetime for the purpose of water storage, while it was kept dry during a siege because a deep moat would have been more difficult to cross than one full of water.

The construction of modern roads has done much harm to the walls, and the incessant traffic noise makes it hard to appreciate some stretches. When in the 1980s international assistance for the restoration of the walls that had been expected from UNESCO failed to materialize, the municipality of Greater Istanbul began restorations in 1986. The first target was the ruined Belgrade Gate (Belgrad Kapısı). Naturally everyone had the best of intentions but the decision to rebuild them was not wise. This section of the walls now looks like a stage-decor, and it would have been better to preserve them in their ruined melancholy state.

Excavation and Restoration of the Walls of Theodosius II

Pipes in wall between 3rd and 4th towers south of 4th military gate towers. Steps on ramp leading to summit of wall

Inner or great wall surmounted by rampart and breastwork also steps on ramp leading to each tower

Top story entered from parapet walk
Middle Story entered from below (wooden floor)
Lowest story entered from city level with communication by means of door at higher level onto inner walk

Line of Inner Towers

Steps on ramp leading to rampart tower

Additional width to rampart

Outer wall with arched and loopholed chambers surmounted by breastwork

Occasional communication is given between inner and outer walks by means of door and passageway–other towers have no lower story

Line of Outer Towers

Scarp surmounted by breastwork

Showing the buttressing to dam walls

Aqueduct
Lower side of 2nd dam wall South of Topkapı (Porta San Romanus)

Counter Scarp

Two 7-inch water pipes
Imbedded into dam wall

Inner Walk

Outer Walk

Scale of Meters

City

Entrance to tower from city
ramp leading from city level to summit of wall

Entrances to towers from city level

Towers of various shapes

Rampart of outer wall
Outer Walk
Scarp surmounted by breastwork
Buttresses
Moat

2-7 inch water pipes
Dam wall

Country

Moat

From the Marmara to the Mevlevihane Gate

> "By the commands of Theodosius, in less than two months, Constantine triumphantly erected these strong walls. Scarcely could Pallas have so quickly built so strong a citadel."
>
> - An inscription above the Mevlevihane Gate

From the Marble Tower to Yedikule Fortress

The Marble Tower stands at the point where the sea and land walls converge, in the southwestern corner of the city. If you cross the coastal road and start walking along the front side of the walls, you will see the first military gate just after the first tower. This is also called the Gate of Christ because of the laureate monogram XP above the doorway. In total there were ten gates in the walls. Five of them were of this type and only gave access to the outer defenses, while the other public gates connected the city with the outside world by means of bridges.

Follow the track upwards until it crosses the railway line. The orchards make this the most pleasant spot of the walls. The moat, today filled with kitchen gardens, is at its deepest here, and you can judge for yourself how difficult it would have been for the enemy to cross it. The Fort of the Seven Towers (Yedikule), built at one of the highest points of the walled city, rises upwards. The Yedikule Fortress is a huge pentagonal structure, consisting of both Turkish and Byzantine constructions, the latter made up of the Theodosian walls with the Golden Gate. In Ottoman times one of the Yedikule towers was mainly used as a prison for important personages. Today it is a museum and the castle's lush courtyard is a little oasis in the city.

The Golden Gate can only be accessed from inside the museum. Across from the entrance there is a wooden door which leads to the outer courtyard and gate. The gate consists of three archways and is flanked by two square marble towers. Two imperial Byzantine eagles are still visible at the corner of each tower. There is a sundial on the south wall of the left tower, but it is becoming more difficult to read with each coming year.

The Porta Aura was the ceremonial gate through which victorious emperors and generals rode into the city. The principal captives, divided into several companies and guarded by bands of soldiers, led the march. Next followed the standards and weapons and other spoils of war. Finally came the Emperor himself, standing in his chariot with his crown on his head, his scepter in his right hand and his victorious sword by his side. Since he always had to remember that he was a mortal, he dismounted at the gate and prostrated himself to humbly acknowledge that he owed his victory only to the all-powerful God. When the Emperor entered the city, the circus factions heralded the Emperor, cheering, "Glory to God, who has magnified you, Emperors of the Romans, Glory to Thee, All-Holy Trinity, for we behold our Emperors victorious." The ostentatious procession then wended its way to the Great Palace, through the dense crowds that packed the main thoroughfare of ancient Constantinople, all gay with banners, flowers and evergreens.

The Golden Gate was most probably constructed during the reign of Theodosius I and thus stood outside the city walls. On the Golden Gate there was an inscription in gilded bronze letters (the holes for these letters are still visible on the central arch) which read:

"*Theodosius adorns this gate after the suppression of the Tyrant: the builder of this Gate of God brings back the Golden Age.*"

Its large open gateways were not successful as defense, even if one assumes that they could be closed by huge doors. So when the land walls were built they constructed an outer gateway to make it more defensible. The huge gates were already walled up by the tenth century, and perhaps even earlier.

If you tip the caretaker, he will provide the key (*anahtar*) for the marble tower to the left of the Golden Gate. Its terrace provides a view of the entire city and the Theodosian wall strutting toward the Golden Horn.

This is one of the finest views in the city and should not be missed.

An Exciting Stroll

This walk will cost some effort and although it is not dangerous should not be attempted by those who have a fear of heights. First go from the museum to the gate you passed through from outside the walls. It was here that Basil, the founder of the Macedonian Dynasty, entered the city as a homeless adventurer in search of fortune (see the introduction). Walk behind the restaurant on the left and climb up onto the inner wall. This may appear a pretty hazardous undertaking, but it is not for there is a little walking track on top. These walls are a source of constant delight to the Byzantine scholar since there are many inscriptions found here at several points referring to the renovation of the walls. At the breach in the walls, go down and take the path that leads through the kitchen gardens along the inside of the wall or walk, when the fields are too muddy, in front of the wall. The path leads to the Belgrade Gate, the gate that was rebuilt in such a theatrical fashion.

From this gate on you can walk between the outer and inner walls. The next public entrance into the city was Silivri Gate. In the Byzantine era it was usually referred to as the Gate of Pege because it led to one of the most venerable shrines of Byzantium, Zoodochus Pege, or the Life-Giving Spring.

If the gate on the right hand side, just before the bridge over the moat at Silivri Gate is not locked, you can continue walking between the inner and outer

The Fish Church

With its healing waters and shrines, its cypress groves and meadows it was a popular resort area. Here the emperors had a palace and hunting grounds to which they often retired. The present chapel was built in 1833, but the subterranean crypt is Byzantine. The Turks called it the Fish Church because of the following tale. On the day of the Conquest a monk was frying some fish near the holy spring. When someone told him that the city had fallen to the infidel he exclaimed in disbelief, "I will only believe this if these fish jump out of the pan into the water," and that is of course exactly what they did. The fish—allegedly gold on one side and black on the other—now gliding in the dim recesses of the *ayazma* are considered the lineal descendants of their half-fried ancestry. The outer courtyard contains an old tombstone in the Karamanlı script (Turkish written in the Greek alphabet). The inner courtyard is filled with tombs of bishops and patriarchs. Each is seated in his tomb on a throne; the monument rising above each grave is shaped like an altar and adorned with the Byzantine double-headed eagle.

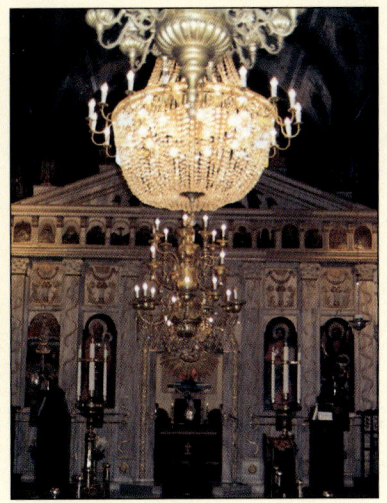

walls and have a look at a curious structure that was recently discovered, a late fifth century Roman burial chamber. The crypt contains beautifully carved tombs. The attire of the figures leads us to understand that the Roman influence was still predominant at that time; in late Byzantine times clothing styles were more eastern looking.

Our walk ends at the Mevlevihane Gate, named after the dervish lodge that once stood outside the walls. In Byzantine times this gate was called the Gate of Rhegium or the Gate of the Red Faction, after one of the circus parties of the Hippodrome. The inscription quoted in the beginning of this chapter was placed on the corbel of the outer gate.

From the Edirne Gate to the Golden Horn

On this enjoyable walk we will explore Byzantine palaces, churches, dungeons, holy wells and neighborhoods with a very rural atmosphere.

From the Edirne Gate to the Tekfur Palace

The Edirne Gate or Porta Adrianopolis (as Edirne was called in ancient days) stands at the highest point of the city, 77 meters above sea level. It was through this gate that the Sultan made his triumphal entry when the city was finally conquered. A little further down the road, in the direction of the center of town, lies the open cistern of Aetios that is now in use as a sports stadium.

If you cross Fevzipaşa Caddesi and continue to walk along the inside of the Theodosian walls, you will come automatically to a wonderful Byzantine building, the Palace of Porphyrogenitus (those that were born into the purple). Today it is better known as Tekfur Palace, from a Persian word signifying the wearer of the crown. Its striking ornamental façade, with its geometric patterns in brick and colored marbles, attests to the ori-

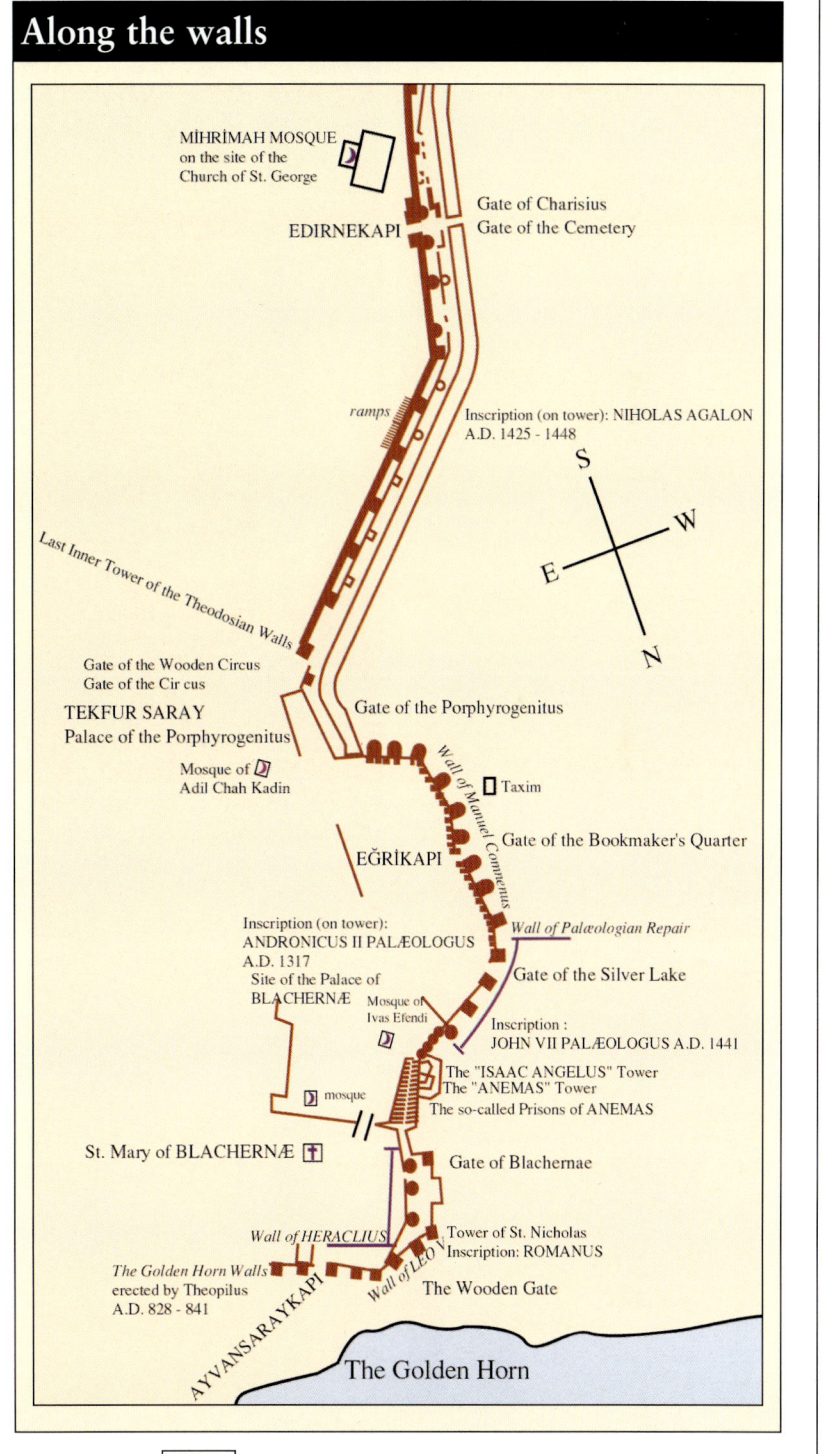

Along the walls

MİHRİMAH MOSQUE on the site of the Church of St. George

EDİRNEKAPI

Gate of Charisius
Gate of the Cemetery

ramps

Inscription (on tower): NIHOLAS AGALON A.D. 1425 - 1448

Last Inner Tower of the Theodosian Walls

Gate of the Wooden Circus
Gate of the Circus

TEKFUR SARAY
Palace of the Porphyrogenitus

Mosque of Adil Chah Kadin

Gate of the Porphyrogenitus

Wall of Manuel Comnenus

Taxim

Gate of the Bookmaker's Quarter

EĞRİKAPI

Inscription (on tower):
ANDRONICUS II PALÆOLOGUS
A.D. 1317
Site of the Palace of BLACHERNÆ

Mosque of Ivas Efendi

Wall of Palæologian Repair

Gate of the Silver Lake

Inscription :
JOHN VII PALÆOLOGUS A.D. 1441

mosque

The "ISAAC ANGELUS" Tower
The "ANEMAS" Tower
The so-called Prisons of ANEMAS

St. Mary of BLACHERNÆ

Gate of Blachernae

Wall of HERACLIUS

Tower of St. Nicholas
Inscription: ROMANUS

The Golden Horn Walls erected by Theopilus A.D. 828 - 841

AYVANSARAYKAPI

Wall of LEO

The Wooden Gate

The Golden Horn

61

ental influence that had begun to have a growing effect on Byzantine decorative art from the tenth century onwards. The palace was built somewhere in the twelfth or thirteenth century, possibly as an extension to the nearby Blachernae Palace. This part of the city became very fashionable in the Paleologian era when the rich established churches and mansions along the high ridge. It is said that the palace location gave it a strategic importance, allowing the imperial guard to double as defenders of the city.

If the gate is locked, there is a way in for the adventurous. Climb up the wall at the back. From there you can walk to the tower, which is not very difficult to scale, since I made it up here with enterprising seventy year olds, but if you have a fear of heights it is best not to try. The view from above is marvelous; you can see both the Golden Horn and the twelfth century Comnenian walls.

Stonework of the Tekfur Palace

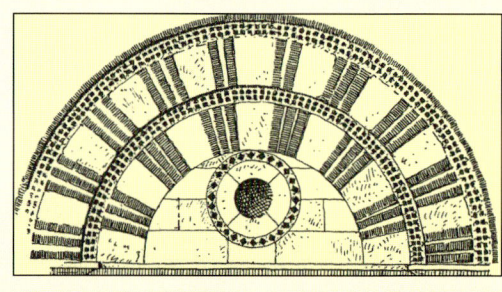

The Wall of Comnenus and Ayvansaray

The walls of Theodosius ends at this gate. The fortifications now continue with a single wall erected by Emperor Manuel Comnenus (1143-80) for the defense of the Blachernae Palace. A moat was not deemed necessary since the slope is very steep. To make up for this deficiency the wall was built thicker and flanked by stronger towers, higher and closer together than on any other section of the enceinte. In front of these walls lies a picturesque Christian graveyard (the gate-keeper will let you in).

Below the Tekfur Palace is another gate in the wall, the Eğri Kapı or the Crooked Gate. It was here that the Byzantine Emperor was last seen alive on the final day of the siege. Follow the street that leads upward winding its way through little gardens. Up ahead you will see the sixteenth century İvaz Efendi Mosque. The mosque is our goal since it is the site of the Blachernae Palace, the favorite residence of the imperial court in the twelfth century. It stood on an artificially terraced hill and foreign visitors could not find words to give an idea of its magnificence and wealth. The area has not been excavated and there must be a great deal to be found under the dilapidated Turkish houses of this ancient district.

The huge substructures below the mosque are very impressive but before looking at them you can enjoy the view from the towers that were once a part of the palace. The one to the left is called the Tower of Isaac Angelus and it served as a belvedere. The tower to the right is called the Tower of Anemas and was used as a prison, where many were killed and mutilated.

A modern concrete stairway in the terrace gives access to the dungeons, but nowadays you have to walk out of the mosque's courtyard and go to the nearby abandoned teahouse. There you will find the stairs that lead to the dungeons. Be sure to bring your own flashlight. The arched tunnel of the basement is 60 meters long and two to twelve meters wide. Because the wooden floors no longer exist, these structures give an impression of immense height.

The street downhill leads to two parallel walls. The Heraclian inner wall was constructed in 627 to protect the quarter of Blachernae. The fortifications here are flanked by three fine hexagonal towers, built toward their summit in brick to lighten the weight of constructions erected on marshy grounds. In 813 Leo V erected the outer wall as an extra defense.

The neighborhood along this part of the Golden Horn is now called Ayvansaray, a name derived from the Persian word *eyvan* denoting a tall building with great arches, obviously the Blachernae Palace. The iron gate opposite the local teahouse gives entrance to the famous Blachernae Ayazma. Holy springs (*ayazma*) are the least known Byzantine monuments of the city and there are quite a number of them to be found. This spring was particularly famous since it housed the relics of the Virgin. In Byzantine times it was a little Lourdes where the Emperor and the Empress came to partake of its life-giving waters. The water is still believed to be curative. The present-day chapel dates from the nineteenth century. You can go inside and drink some of the water but be sure to leave a small donation. The priest here might even want to sing a hymn for you. Again a donation is expected. It is a place full of melancholic charm. On Saturdays no more than a dozen elderly believers still gather here to honor the Holy Mother of God.

The Dungeon of the Blachernae Palace

The vicissitudes of the inmates occupying the Blachernae Dungeon reflect the complex nature of Byzantine society with its strange mixture of good and evil—cruel, atrocious and decadent, yet also capable of grandeur, energy and effort, genuine piety and compassion.

The Tower of Anemas was named after a nobleman of Arabian descent. When the Byzantines recaptured Crete, the Emir and his family were paraded through the streets of Constantinople. Somehow the dignity of their demeanor left a most favorable impression on the spectators. The Emperor made a magnanimous gesture and allowed the Emir to spend his days on an estate, surrounded by his friends and unmolested on account of his faith. His descendants embraced Christianity and many made careers in the imperial army. One of them, a young aristocrat named Michael Anemas, was, however, so unfortunate as to become involved in a conspiracy against Emperor Alexius Comnenus (1081-1118). Upon discovery of the plot Michael Anemas, dressed in sacking, was dragged through the streets with his beard plucked out, his head shorn and crowned with the horns of an ox and the intestines of a sheep. The agony of Michael, as he implored to be put to death rather than to be blinded, touched all hearts and his pitiful appearance excited commiseration rather than ridicule. Overwhelmed with tears the Empress hastened back to the palace, prevailing upon Alexius to spare the prisoner's sight. The Emperor conceded and Anemas was saved from his horrible fate at the very last moment. He was then imprisoned in the tower, which was to perpetuate his name. At length Michael even received a pardon.

The most famous inmate of the tower was Emperor Andronicus Comnenus (1183-1185). He was already sixty-five years old when he became Emperor but in spite of his years he had preserved the good looks and the energy of a young man. His wit, panache and the fame of his almost legendary exploits in bed, as well as on the battlefield, won him an unrivaled reputation. Occupying the throne however did not make him a better man. Now that he had achieved his lifetime ambition, all kinds of hidden vices, like cruelty, suspicion and brutality came out. Large-scale persecutions were issued until every citizen was afraid that they would hear a knock on the door. When this mini-Stalin ordered the mass execution of all prisoners and boasted—of all places—in the Hagia Sophia that he had murdered his nephew who was thought to harbor imperial ambitions, the people revolted. Andronicus was reviled, beaten, struck on the mouth and had his hair and beard plucked out. They poured buckets of boiling water over his head, cut off one of his hands and then left him in the Anemas dungeon for days without food or water. Finally Andronicus was sentenced in the Hippodrome, hanged by the feet on an architrave of two columns that stood beside the statues of a wolf and a hyena, his natural associates. The captive repeated the words, "Kyrie Eleison, Why dost Thou break the bruised reed over and over again," but his words did not excite the slightest commiseration. Finally three men plunged their swords into his body, only to exhibit their dexterity in arms, and brought his agony to an end.

His successor, Isaac Angelus (1185-1195), shared the same fate. He was incarcerated in the dungeon after being blinded, which seems to have been the classical Byzantine disfiguration of deposed emperors. His imprisonment was a reason for his son to seek help abroad to restore his father to the throne, thus giving the Crusaders the pretext they needed to invade Byzantine territory. Isaac was briefly restored to the throne in 1213, ruling as co-emperor with his son. Father and son were strangled in the Anemas dungeon because they had tried to bring the Orthodox Church back into the Latin fold and had delivered the capital to the Crusaders.

The Chora Church (Kariye Mosque)

While the Hagia Sophia commands respect through the sheer magnitude of its size, the Chora Church impresses through the beauty of its brilliant mosaics and frescoes. Byzantine art can be rigid at times, but here we see a new style emerging, full of pathos, ecstasy, warmth and intimacy. This is a site that must be seen on any trip to Istanbul.

History

Chora means "in the country," so it is supposed that at the time of its founding the church stood outside the city walls. Excavations, however, did not reveal any substructure younger than the sixth century. Therefore it is better to ascribe a mystical meaning to the name, for after all the Byzantines lived in a universe in which everything carried meaning. In some of the inscriptions that accompany the mosaics, Christ and the Mother of God are called Chora, meaning the dwelling place or land of the living. Many churches were dedicated to Christ or the Mother of God in one or another attributes by which they were known: Christ as the Akataleptos (Incompressible), Dynamis (All-powerful), Evergetes (Benefactor), Pantocrator (Omnipotent); the Mother of God as Elousa (Merciful), Pammakaristos (All-blessed), Panachrantos (All-pure).

The present-day structure dates back to the beginning of the twelfth century but most of what we see now, the two narthexes and the side chapel, date from the years 1315-1321 when the church was rebuilt and redecorated by the Grand Logothete (the Treasury Minister), Theodore Metochites. Metochites was a typical product of Paleologian times. He thought of himself and his compatriots as Hellenes and was immensely proud of the Greek heritage. He recommended his pupils read the ancient philosophers, including the Skeptics for, he remarked, all human wisdom that is based on experience can be challenged by arguments based on contrary experience. The study of history should not be left out, because it shows us how varied human experience can be. Such enlightening words could only come from a great humanistic thinker and were typical for that age. With the downfall of his Emperor Andronicus II (1282-1328), Metochites fell from grace too, but was allowed to live in his beloved monastery of the Chora, with all the reminders of his past fame and fortunes. Metochites died here in 1332, a little more than one hundred years before the final end of the Empire.

The church was converted into a mosque in the early sixteenth century and the mosaics were then covered with plaster. The frescoes and mosaics were totally restored by Professor Whittemore and Paul Underwood from 1948 to 1958.

The Evangelical Cycles

The Paleologian artist did not want to create icons but to recall the workings of the divine on earth in the form of a huge picture book. As a result the walls of the churches in Paleologian times were covered by evangelical cycles that became more and more extensive, as people wanted to know more and more about the Holy Family. This is the reason why we see the childhood of Mary depicted in the Chora Church. This story, which was extremely popular in medieval times, finds its origin in the apocryphal gospel of St. James which was written in Egypt in the second century. The author did not want only to provide more information about the Holy Family but also wanted to prove that Mary had always been a virgin and was never defiled. The delicate point was that Mark (6:3) and Matthew (13:55) mention that the Lord had brothers and sisters. The logical conclusion that Joseph had taken Mary to his bed after she had begotten the Saviour was for many people a particular abhorrent thought as they thought of Joseph as a widower who already had children. The book of St. James tells us that he did not fancy taking Mary to his home since he feared that he would be the laughing stock to the children of Israel. In medieval times the story was enacted on the stage in England. When this episode came, Joseph exclaimed:

> *Her warden and her keeper will I ever be...*
> *In bed we shall never meet*
> *For I know, maiden sweet*
> *An old man cannot rage*

So Joachim and Anna found their way onto the stage. It is safe to say that no other apocryphal gospel had a greater influence. It became the source of the cult of Saint Anne and the Feast of the Presentation of the Virgin in the Temple, and the inspiration of many of the masterpieces from Italian painters such as Giotto, Raphael and Titian.

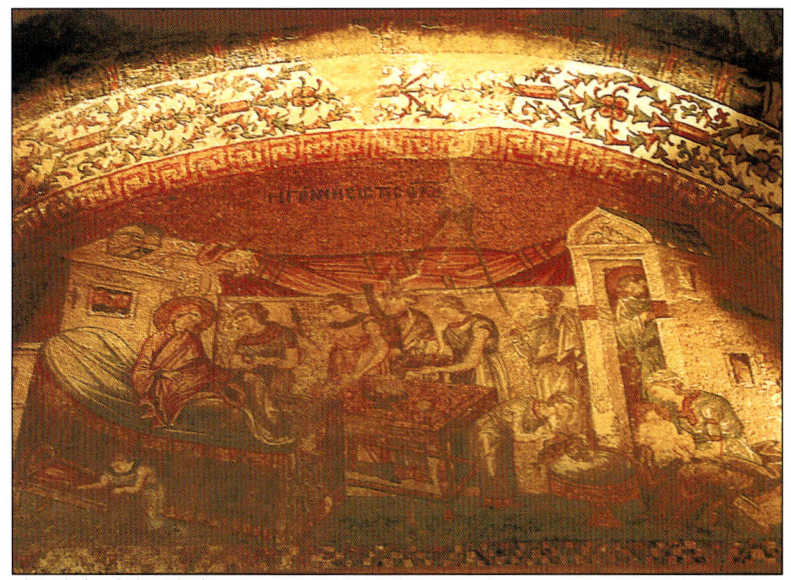

The Geneology of Christ

The Birth of the Virgin

Dedicatory and Devotional Panels

1. Christ Pantocrator

The first of the mosaics confronting the visitor upon entering the church is the monumental image of Christ the Pantocrator. Christ no longer has the stern appearance of earlier times, but is seen as a gentler person. This Pantocrator type is very important to the Orthodox, who prefer to adore Christ as a victorious and triumphant king rather than to depict Him, as was done in the West, as the man of sorrows hanging on the Cross.

2. The Theotokos (Mother of God) with Angels

Opposite the Pantocrator is the Virgin with her hands outstretched in prayer. The inscription describes the Virgin as "chora tou achoretouí" meaning that the Godhead who could not be "contained" or encompassed, as a finite being was nevertheless "contained" through the incarnation. The reference to this mysterious happening is visually demonstrated in the mosaic, since the Christ child appears in an aureole on her breast.

3. Christ Enthroned and the Donor

This panel shows Theodore Metochites offering a model of his beloved church to Christ. He is dressed in a kind of caftan, on his head he wears a silk *skiadion* (literally, sunshade). There could be no greater difference in appearance between this man and his Roman colleagues in early Byzantine times who looked very Roman in their togas. As the centuries advanced clothes grew more elaborate: elaborate headdresses were worn by both sexes and a beard was considered a sign of culture. To shave the chin was Western and vulgar.

4./5. St. Peter and St. Paul

On either side of the door to the nave we can see Peter, the "Rock" on which the Church was founded, and Paul, the great teacher.

6. The Deesis

A Deesis panel normally portrays Christ flanked by the Mother of God and John the Baptist; however, this time the Baptist has been omitted. On the side of the Virgin is Prince Isaac Comnenus, who was probably responsible for the rebuilding of the church in the twelfth century. On Christ's side is a depiction of the Lady of the Mongols who founded the still extant church of St. Mary of the Mongols in Fener.

7./8. The Genealogy of Christ
Southern and Northern Dome

The main purpose of the mosaics of the southern dome (Christ Pantocrator and His ancestors) and the northern dome (the Virgin with sixteen kings in the house of David) is to commemorate the ancestors of Christ and the Virgin as the lineage through whom the Word was made flesh and the divine plan of salvation carried out.

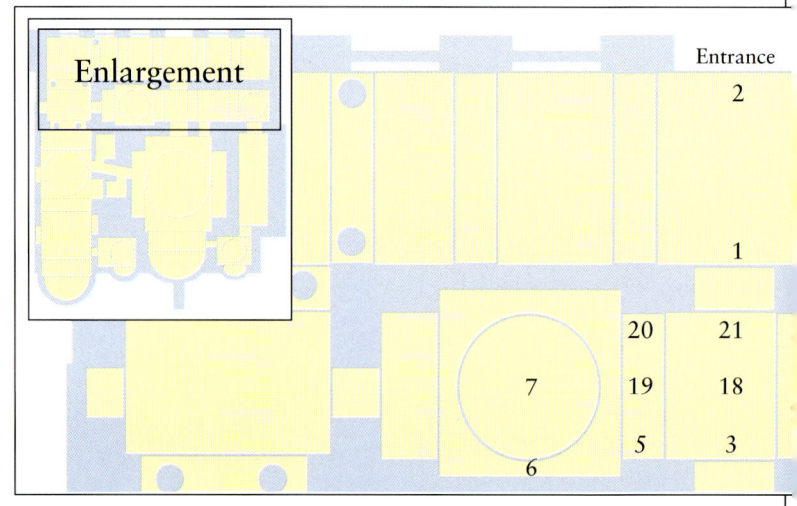

The Life of the Virgin

9. Joachim's Offerings Rejected

This panel begins the story of Joachim told through a series of panels. He and his wife were exceedingly rich, but unhappy because they bore no children. When they came to the temple, Zacharias (the only figure you see) refused them entry.

10. Partially Destroyed

A maidservant peering out from a doorway.

11. Joachim Praying in the Wilderness

The story goes on: "And Joachim was sore grieved, and showed himself to his wife, but betook himself to the wilderness and fasted forty days and nights."

Dedicatory and Devotional 1-8
The Life of the Virgin 9-27

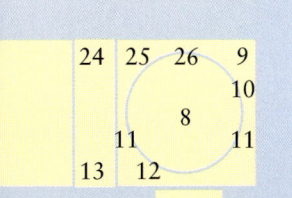

12. The Annunciation to St. Anne

Back home, Anne was not happy either. When she walked in her garden and saw two little birds nesting in the trees, she broke down in tears and lamented, "Unto what am I likened, since the fowls of heaven and the beasts of the earth are all fruitful before the lord and better of then me." Then an Angel appeared who told her that God heard her prayer and that her seed should be spoken of through the whole world. In return Anne promised that she would give the child to the Lord's service.

13. The Conception of the Mother of God

This scene represents the conception of the Mother of the God-bearer. This joyful event is still celebrated in the Orthodox Church on the ninth day of December. The tenderness that is expressed by the embrace of Joachim and Anne is also to be found in the following scenes and reflects the interest that the Paleologian artist took in depicting people and their emotions.

14. The Birth of the Mother of God

The birth of the Virgin is celebrated in the Church on September 8.

15. She Who Takes Seven Steps

The Gospel of St. John tells us: "And day by day the child waxed strong, and when she was six months old her mother stood her upon the ground to try if she would stand; and she walked seven steps and returned unto her bosom. And she caught her up, saying: As the Lord my God liveth, thou shalt walk no more upon this ground, until I bring thee into the temple of the Lord." From that moment on the Gospel informs us she was carried everywhere. Through this strange story the author wanted to emphasise the purity of the Virgin.

The way the panel is executed is also of interest. The billowing scarf of the maidservant doesn't have a symbolic meaning, it is just there because the artist took delight in this decorative feature. This is a good example of the renewed interest in the motifs and styles that were in vogue in late classical antiquity.

16. The Blessing of the Priests

Joachim celebrated Mary's first birthday with a great feast to which he invited the priests, scribes and all Israel.

17. The Caressing of Theotokos

A tender scene with no foundation in the textual sources. Note the peacocks, symbol of immortality.

18. The Holy of Holiest

When Mary was three years old, Ann and Joachim presented her to the temple where she served until she was twelve.

19. The Virgin Receiving Bread from an Angel

During her stay in the temple Mary was nurtured with heavenly food.

20. Destroyed

Only the architectural setting remains from this scene.

21. The Virgin Receiving a Skein of Purple Wool

The Evangelium says: "Now there was a council of the priests, and they said: Let us make a veil for the temple of the Lord. And the priest said: Call unto me pure virgins of the tribe of David. (...) and the priest said: Cast me lots, which of you shall weave the gold and the undefiled (white) and the fine linen and the silk and the hyacinthine, and the scarlet and the purple. And the lot of the true purple and the scarlet [the royal colors] fell unto Mary."

22. The Prayer before the Rods

When the time came for the Virgin to be married, an Angel instructed Zacharias to go forth and assemble the widowers of Israel. Mary sits before the twelve rods (symbol of the twelve tribes of Israel) and Zacharias prays before the altar.

23. The Handing over to Joseph

It was the rod of Joseph that began to sprout. Zacharias told him that he had to take the Virgin to his house although Joseph initially refused.

24. Joseph, Taking the Mother of God to his House

The youthful son of Joseph looks rather suspiciously at Mary walking behind his father.

25. The Annunciation at the Well

The Handing Over to Joseph

An Angel came to Mary and said: "Hail, thou that are highly favored, blessed are thou among women." The artist was here very successful in capturing Mary's surprise.

26. Joseph Taking Leave of the Virgin

Joseph left to build his buildings. When came back he found his wife pregnant and quite understandably wept bitterly and accused her saying "Mary, what is this thy deed?" The dead root of a tree that has put forth a living branch is symbolic.

27. Joseph Reproaching the Virgin

Destroyed.

The Infancy of Christ

From now on most scenes are based on verses from the canonical Gospels

1. **Joseph Dreaming and the Journey to Bethlehem**

First we see that Joseph has a dream in which an Angel reassures him "that which is conceived in Mary is of the Holy Ghost." The journey to Bethlehem is depicted particularly vividly, with a donkey that seems to dance and figures that appear to float over the ground.

2. **The Enrollment for Taxation**

Cyrenius, governor of Syria, sits on his throne supervising the enrollment, and is questioning Mary, who is depicted as an unusually tall figure. Joseph with his sons stands behind her.

3. **The Birth of Christ**

Folkloric legends are clearly seen in the reference to the cave as the site of the divine birth. This was a common motif far earlier that the Christian legend. The mosaic is a composite of a number of incidents connected with the birth of Christ. Joseph is gazing at the Christ child as if he still does not believe what the Angel told him.

4. **The Journey of the Wise Men & The Wise Men before Herod**

The inscription refers to Matthew (2:1-2), "And behold, there came wise men from the East to Jerusalem, saying 'Where is he who is brought forth King of the Jews?'"

5. **Herod inquiring Where Christ Was**

6. **The Flight to Egypt**

As the Holy Family escaped to Egypt, idols fell from the walls of the towns they passed (from an apocryphal source).

7. **The Massacre of the Innocents**

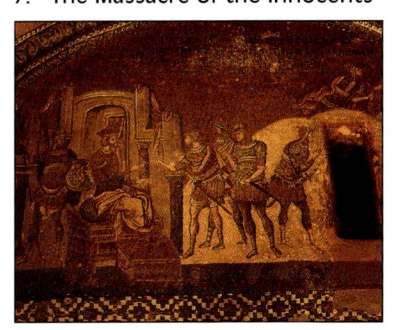

Herod orders the soldiers to kill all the babies.

8. **Soldiers Slaying the Children**

9. **Mothers Mourning their Children**

10. **The Flight of Elizabeth**

This panel is based on a verse in the apocryphal gospel of St. James, and depicts Elizabeth with her baby son St. John the Baptist. They were swallowed by a mountain in order to protect them from Roman soldiers who were in hot pursuit.

11. **The Return to Nazareth**

An Angel again appears to Joseph in a dream telling him that Nazareth is the safest place for them to go (Matt 2:22-23).

12. **Christ Taken to Jerusalem for the Passover**

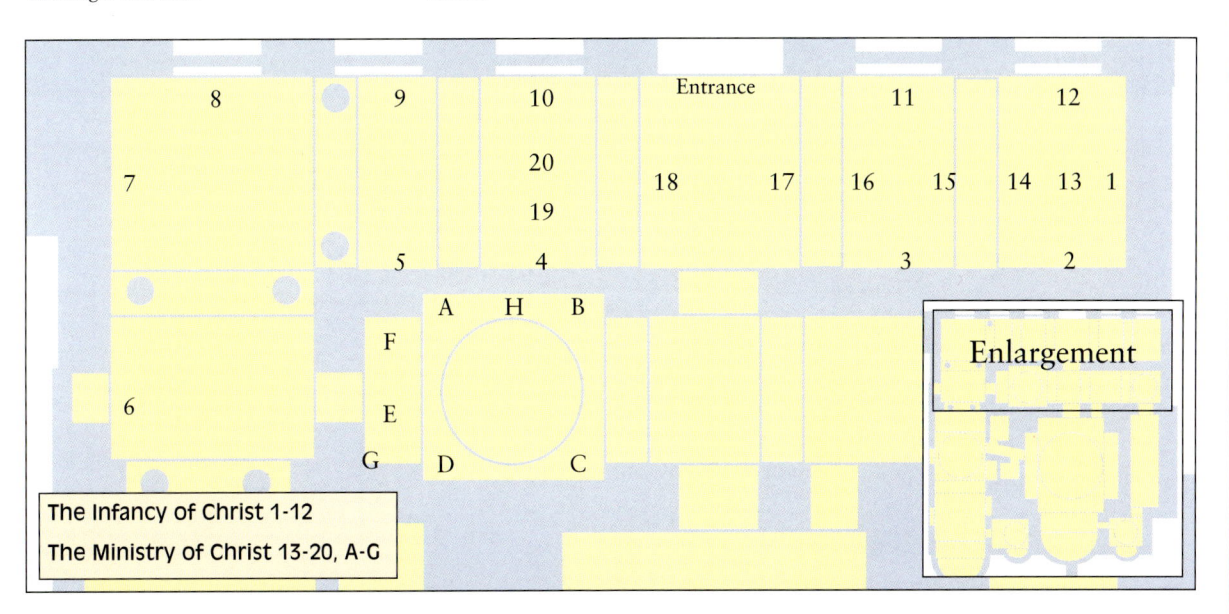

The Infancy of Christ 1-12
The Ministry of Christ 13-20, A-G

Christ's Ministry and the Nave Mosaics

13. Christ Among the Teachers

Nearly totally destroyed.

14. John the Baptist Bearing Witness to Christ

Only fragments remain.

15. John the Baptist Bearing Witness to Christ

This scene is clearly visible in the dome. "This is he, of whom I said, 'He who comes after me ranks before me, for he was before me '"(John 1, 15 & 30).

16. The Temptations of Christ (Matt. 4:3-7)

Devil: If thou be the Son of God, command that these stones be bread.
Christ: It is written, Man shall not live by bread alone, but by every word that proceedeth out of the mouth of God.
Devil: All these things will I give thee, if thou wilt fall down and worship me
Christ: Go away Satan.
Devil: Then the Adversary is taking Him along into the holy city, and stands Him to the wing of the sanctuary.
Devil: If you are the Son of God, cast yourself down.
Christ: It is written .... Thou shalt not tempt the Lord thy God.

17. The Miracle at Cana 1

The scene of the changing of the water into wine is preserved (John 2: 10).

18. The Miracle at Cana 2

The center is lost. We see Christ giving the multiplied bread to two disciples beneath whom a group of children eat: on the other side there is Christ and some of the 5000. (Based on Matthew 14:15-21 also in other gospels.)

19. Christ Healing a Leper

Only the legs of the Leper with his ulcers can still be seen.

20. Christ Walking on Water

This is hardly visible. The vaults of the fifth, sixth and seventh bays have lost nearly all their mosaics.

CHRIST'S MIRACLES OF HEALING

A. The Blind and Dumb Man (Matt. 12: 22)

B. The Two Blind Men (Matt. 20: 29-30).

C. Peter's Mother-in-law (Matt. 8:14-15).

John and Andrew Stand beside Him

D. The Women With the Issue of Blood (Matt. 9:20-22).

E. The Man with the Withered Hand (Matt. 12: 9-13).

F. The Leper (Matt. 8:2-3).
Very vividly drawn!

G. Unidentified Act of Healing

H. Christ Healing a Multitude (Matt. 15:30).

The Nave Mosaics

The Dormition (Koimesis) of the Virgin.
The dormition of the Virgin is an important feast in the Orthodox Church (15 Aug). In the West it is celebrated as Ascension Day. The Virgin lies dead on her bier, surrounded by the apostles and early bishops. Behind her stands Christ holding her soul as a baby in His hands. Above hovers a six-winged seraph, symbolizing the entrance to Paradise.

Christ (not shown)

The Virgin Hodegetria (right)
She who points the way.

The Frescoes of the Funerary Chapel

All scenes here refer to redemption and resurrection because the side chapel of the Chora was intended for funerary purposes. The use of the brush made it easier for the Paleologian artist to depict the emotions that he so eagerly wanted to express.

1. **The Anastasis (The Resurrection)**

While in the West the Resurrection was represented by the women who discovered the empty tomb, the Orthodox Church chose the far more dramatic story told in the apocryphal gospel of Nicodemus. A great voice of thunder is heard in hell that Christ, the King of Glory, is coming. Hades orders his devils to prepare the defense. When the voice speaks again it commands, "Lift up the gates" and the gates are then broken while the dead are loosed from their bonds. Christ commands angels to bind Satan and charges Hades to hold Satan until his Second Coming. Then he raises Adam and Eve from the grave as a sign of the redemption of the righteous.

2. **Christ Resurrecting the Widow's Son (Luke 7:11-15).**

3. **Christ Resurrecting Jarius' Daughter (Mark 5:22-24, 35-43).**

4. **The Second Coming of Christ**

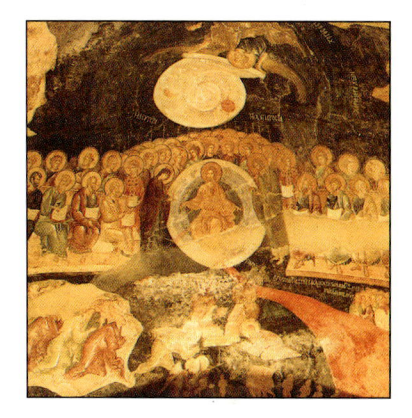

This composite scene occupies the whole vault. In the center is something that looks like a snail shell but it is in fact the scroll of heaven. The scene refers to the Apocalypse 6:14 where it states that "the heaven departed as a scroll which is rolled together." As is to be expected the most prominent position is given to Christ in judgment. As usual the Virgin and John the Baptist stand by His side as intercessors on behalf of mankind. To the left and right of them sit the twelve apostles, and between them and hell is the weighing of souls. A balance is suspended from the foot of the throne and under it stands men, with arms folded, awaiting judgment. In the next scene the condemned are led to the lake of fire.

5. **The Land and Sea Releasing their Dead**

Difficult to see.

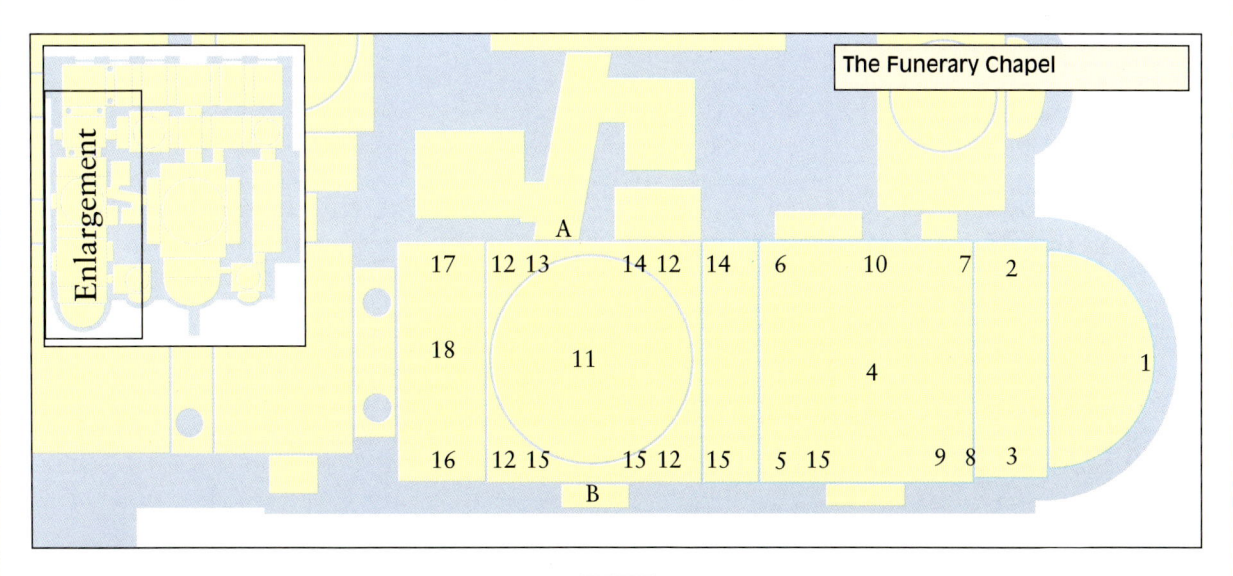

6. An Angel and a Soul

7. Lazarus the Beggar in Abraham's Bsom

8. The Rich Man in Hell

9. The Torments of the Damned

The dark blue one (upper right):
    The outer darkness
The light brown one (upper left):
    The gnashing of teeth (hardly visible)
The dark blue one (lower left):
    The worm that sleepeth not
The red one (lower right):
    The unquenchable fire

10. The Elect Enter Paradise

St. Peter leads the elect to the gate of Paradise, on which a Cherub is depicted. The good thief (who was crucified the same time as Jesus) points toward the Virgin.

THE PREFIGURATIONS OF MARY

11. The Virgin and Child Surrounded by Angels

12. Four Hymnographers

13. Jacob's Ladder: Jacob Wrestling with the Angel

The objects through which God made manifest his presence, in this case the ladder reaching to heaven, were regarded as the Virgin in a variety of forms. This may appear far-fetched but for the religious mind of the Byzantine nothing was impossible. Perhaps the ladder is a prefiguration of the Virgin symbolizing the bridge between men and God.

The Virgin and Child Surrounded by Angels

14. Moses and the Burning Bush

Like the Ladder of Jacob, the burning bush is a symbol of the Mother of God. Here it alludes to the virgin birth, for as the burnting bush was not consumed, so Mary gave birth but remained undefiled.

15. The Bearing of the Ark of the Covenant and the installation in the Temple

The Ark of the Covenant that was brought by Solomon through the temple, was also a container of the uncontainable, and as such is again a prefiguration of the Virgin.

16. Isaiah Prophesying; the Angel Defeating the Assyrians before Jerusalem

The inviolable city Jerusalem is also a symbol of the Virgin.

17. Aaron and his Sons Making Offerings before the Altar

Why the altar is another prefiguration of the Virgin is probably only understood by the Byzantine mind.

18. The Souls of the Righteous in the Hand of God.

Destroyed

All of the saints and martyrs that decorate the walls of the Church cannot be mentioned here, as most of them are almost unknown in the West. The tombs in the niches that are worth mentioning are the tomb of Metochites (A) and that of Michael Tornikes (B), general and beloved friend of Metochites. Strangely enough this tomb is even more elaborately carved than that of Metochites. A long inscription adorns his tomb extolling his virtues as a general and a statesman. The portraits of the deceased were placed on the back wall of the niches, as is the case in the other tombs.

Fener

1. Bulgarian Orthodox Church
2. Old Greek Mansions and Women's Library
3. Patriarchate
4. Greek Lyceum
5. St. Mary of the Mongols
6. Fethiye Mosque (see final chapter)

Fener

Of the districts along the Golden Horn none is more important than the ancient neighborhood of Fener where many Greeks lived in Ottoman times. On this enjoyable walk we will visit the venerable Greek Orthodox Patriarchate, look at dilapidated mansions and climb the step streets of Fener to look at the only church from before the conquest of the city that is still in use as a Christian place of worship.

On the Shores of the Golden Horn

During the Ottoman Empire, a moneyed nobility began to emerge among the enterprising Greeks who built their mansions in Fener to be close to the Patriarchate. Making money, however, was not their prime concern. All the important families claimed imperial descent and their greatest dream was the recreation of the Byzantine Empire. Nowadays the area is not much more than a slum. Squatters from Anatolia occupy the old Greek houses and all but a few are in a sad state of decay. The area has been put under protection and plans are underway for its restoration.

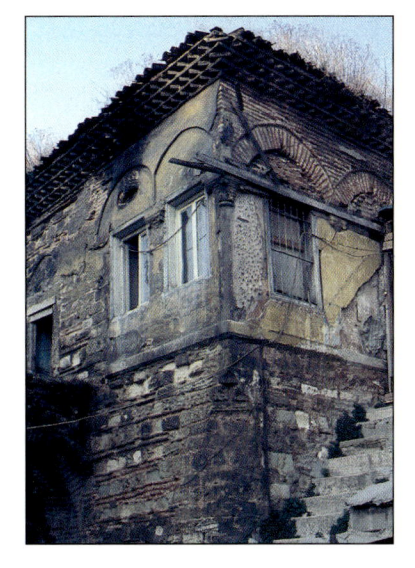

The Bulgarian Orthodox Church of St. Stephen is a curious building crowning this area, but it is not really a Byzantine monument. Approximately 40,000 Bulgarians lived in Constantinople in the mid-nineteenth century, so it was only natural that they petitioned for the right to construct a church. The Ecumenical Patriarchate (in name ecumenical but in fact wholly Greek) responded by ruthlessly imprisoning its leaders on Mount Athos. The Sultan, on the other hand, was more than willing to help the Bulgarians. In 1870 the Bulgarians were given permission by the Sultan to create their own ecclesiastical authority based in Constantinople: the Exarchate. A church was then erected on the shores of the Golden Horn, not accidentally in the vicinity of the Patriarchate. This church was replaced in 1890 by an impressive neo-Gothic building that it is entirely constructed of cast iron. It was cast in Vienna, shipped down the Danube in sections, and then erected here on the shore of the Golden Horn. A caretaker now lives in the exarchate building opposite the entrance gate and will open the door for visitors. Further along, in the middle of the street, are two stoutly built Phanariote mansions. The first mansion is now in ruins. A few decades ago traces of the rococo decoration in the upper room of this house could still be discerned but today everything is gone. The next mansion fared better for it was recently totally restored and is now in use as a women's library and information center (Kadın Eserleri Kütüphanesi).

The Greeks under Ottoman Dominion

The resentment of the Greeks against Rome ran so deep that some thought it better to live under the Turkish turban than the Latin miter. It may therefore come as no surprise that Mehmet IV, the conqueror of Constantinople, and Gennadius, the new Patriarch, got along quite well. It has to be remembered that the Sultan was—unlike many of his successors—a well-educated man who was deeply interested in Greek learning. He was not hostile to the well-being of the Greeks. The Sultan realized that if he kept them content their commercial talent could only contribute to the prosperity of his Empire. As people of the Book, who "it was believed" had known a previous but incomplete stage of revelation, the Christians were treated by the Ottoman government with respect. They did have to receive official permission before being allowed to build or repair churches and for much of the Empire they, like all of the citizens of the Empire, had to wear clothing distinctive to their ethnicity and social class. As long as they behaved like loyal citizens, though, they were allowed to govern their own affairs, and could obtain high positions at the Ottoman court without having to forsake their beliefs. Ironically the Greeks profited from the rebirth of the capital under Ottoman rule. At the time of the conquest the population numbered fewer than 50,000 while a hundred years later there were 150,000 Greeks living within the walls.

Under Ottoman dominion the church became caught up in a degrading system of corruption and simony. Each new patriarch had to pay heavily for being allowed to take office and because every new appointment brought in more cash, patriarchs were removed and reinstated with kaleidoscopic rapidity. The church may not have fared well during Ottoman times but the rich Phanariotes did. Not content with the shallowness of pure wealth their sons were sent to study at universities in Italy. Many returned as doctors and as such attracted the attention of the sultans. At the end of seventeenth century the Porte decided to create the post of Grand Dragoman for Alexander Mavrocordato, a young Greek doctor and philosopher. Often the function of Dragoman is described as chief translator, but Mavrocordato was a kind of minister of foreign affairs and as such much more important than a humble interpreter. His career opened up new vistas for the ambitious Phanariots whose most ardent wish was to take over the government when Ottoman power finally crumbled. Until that time they were prepared to pledge their alliance to the Sultan and help the Greek people through their influence.

The Greek Orthodox Patriarchate

The big gate of the Greek Orthodox Patriarchate, known by Turks as the Fener Rum Patrikhanesi is further along the street. After the conquest, the Patriarchate was first located in the Church of the Holy Apostles at the site of the present day Fatih Mosque. Since this building was in such a sad state of decay, Gennadius decided to seek shelter in the church Panagia Pammakaristos (nowadays Fethiye Mosque). In 1600 the patriarchal throne was finally installed in the church of St. George at the Phanar. This church acquired its present day shape in the middle of the nineteenth century while the buildings around date from the twentieth century. The Imperial Eagle of Byzantium hangs above the entrance door.

From a purely historical perspective the church is not very exciting, but is worthwhile to see for its beauty and atmosphere. Normally the church is open for visitation until 5 PM, when the vespers start, but one may sit in on these. Sunday mass is at 9:30 AM. Attending mass here will probably make you more aware of the Byzantine spirit than the words of this book ever can as the Orthodox Church mass is a very mystical affair.

The church has two treasures from Byzantine times, the mosaic icon of Panagia Pammakristos (the All-blessed Mother of God) and that of John the Baptist, called the Forerunner. Both are twelfth century works and to be found on the right hand side of the iconostasis. The first mosaic belongs to the Hodegetria type, on which the Mother of God points toward her Son, the Saviour of mankind. The great hermit John is depicted in full length. The miniature portrait of the unknown donor appears in the lower left of the mosaic. There are also three eighteenth century caskets with the holy relics of the female saints Euphemia, Solomone and Theophano (the unbearable first consort of Emperor Leo VI the Wise, see the chapter on the Hagia Sophia). The stone column to which Christ allegedly was bound and whipped is embedded in the wall here. The patriarchal throne is a beautiful work of art made in 1537.

Why the Main Gate of the Patriarchate is Forever Shut

After the conquest there was no emperor left to guide the faithful in worldly matters. This task now fell to the patriarch who in his new role could not avoid being caught up in politics. The biggest problem was a question of loyalty. First of all should the patriarch obey the infidel? This question was difficult but not insoluble. Since Christ had said that one should give Caesar that which was Caesar's, there was nothing really immoral to be found in serving the sultan, as long as he did not meddle with the spiritual affairs of the church. Far trickier was the following problem. The Orthodox faith, being universal, was there for everyone, regardless of race or culture. Gennadius had, when questioned about his nationality, diplomatically stated that he would not call himself a Hellene though he was a Hellene by race, but liked to take his name from his faith. As described above relative to the establishment of the Bulgarian church, the Orthodox church was only theoretically ecumenical. In Ottoman times "Hellenism" and Orthodoxy became inextricably intertwined. This development was to play a major role in the demise of Phanariote ambitions.

In 1821 Alexander Ypsilanti, a Phanariote Prince, invaded Moldavia and called for a general uprising. Many of the Greeks were not pleased with this development because they believed the Ottoman Empire was already in decline and they were in the best position to take it over when it fell. The Sultan took vengeance on the Patriachate, which he suspected of supporting the rebellion, and hanged the Patriarch from the top of the main gate. This is why the main gate is forever shut and painted black. To foster hate among the different communities, his body was given to the Jews to be dragged through their streets at neighboring Balat. Other bishops and laymen were also sent to the gallows, and by the summer that year the great houses in Fener were empty.

Nonetheless there were no large-scale persecutions and the Patriarchate remained in Fener. After all more then 200,000 Greeks lived in the city and their interests could not be overlooked and Greeks still largely administered Turkish government finances. The rich families remained, but now preferred to live along the shores of the Bosphorus, on the Princes' Islands or in the elegant Parisian district of Pera. By the end of the nineteenth century Fener had become a backwater.

Up the Step Street

After passing the Orthodox Church one notices a huge red brick building on the hilltop above. It is often mistaken for the Patriarchate because of its size, but in fact it is the Greek High School built in 1881. The building is proof of the freedom that the Christians enjoyed at the end of the nineteenth century. Until the first decades of that century the presence of non-Muslim structures on the city's skyline was unthinkable. The view from the top of the hill transports us back to the nineteenth century.

Halfway along the stairs is the late seventeenth century mansion of the Greek historian and philosopher, Dimitri Cantemir. This man was virtuous in the ancient sense of the word; he was an excellent all-rounder instead of being just a decent fellow. He wrote an important history paper on the Ottoman Empire, a Greek translation of the Koran, and a treatise on Dualist philosophy. He was a musician too, and published a treatise on Oriental music while at the same time writing bawdy songs. His scholarly interests did not deter him from simultaneously pursuing a political career as the Prince of Moldavia, one of the principalities where the Greeks were allowed by the Sultan to create a little Byzantine universe. Cantemir ended his romantic life in Russia after he had unsuccessfully tried to lead an uprising against the Sultan.

After the step street the road curves around to the left and one sees a delightful church behind a wall; this is the only church built before the conquest that still functions as an Orthodox place of worship. Princess Maria, one of the illegitimate daughters of Michael VIII Palaeologus, (re)built the church around 1282. She was betrothed to the Mongol Khan Abagu who became a Christian through her efforts. When his brother assassinated her husband, she returned to

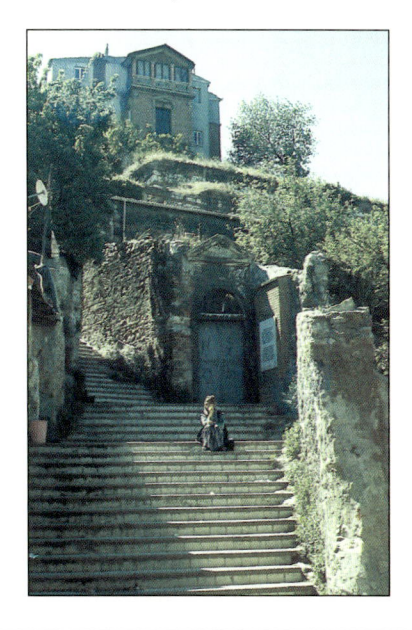

Constantinople, where she retired to the convent whose church was thereafter known, as St. Mary of the Mongols.

There is a moving story connected to the building. Mehmet the Conqueror had employed a Greek architect to build a mosque to be named for him (Fatih Mosque) on the grounds of the dilapidated church of the Holy Apostles. Since the Sultan was pleased with the result, he gave the church of Saint Mary of the Mongols to the mother of the architect because he had heard that she was deeply attached to it. At the end of the seventeenth century the government tried to confiscate the building. However when they were shown the Sultan's original *firman* (an imperial degree in which was stated that the integrity of the church was to be respected), the Grand Vizier kissed it reverently and gave orders that the church was to be unmolested. The original firman can still be seen hanging on the walls, although one wonders why they don't protect this treasure a bit better since it is a document of immense value. The original church was built in a four-leaf clover shape but the entire south side of the church was swept away in the nineteenth century and replaced with a narthex.

Lunch Stop

If you take the whole walk around Fener, you are likely to be starving by this point and may wish to take advantage of an excellent *lokanta* (restaurant) that lies in the vicinity of St. Mary of the Mongols. However, it is best to go to the Kömür Lokantası before lunchtime because if you arrive too late, the workmen who come to eat here may not have left much.

Kömür Lokantası
Near St. Mary of the Mongols, Fener

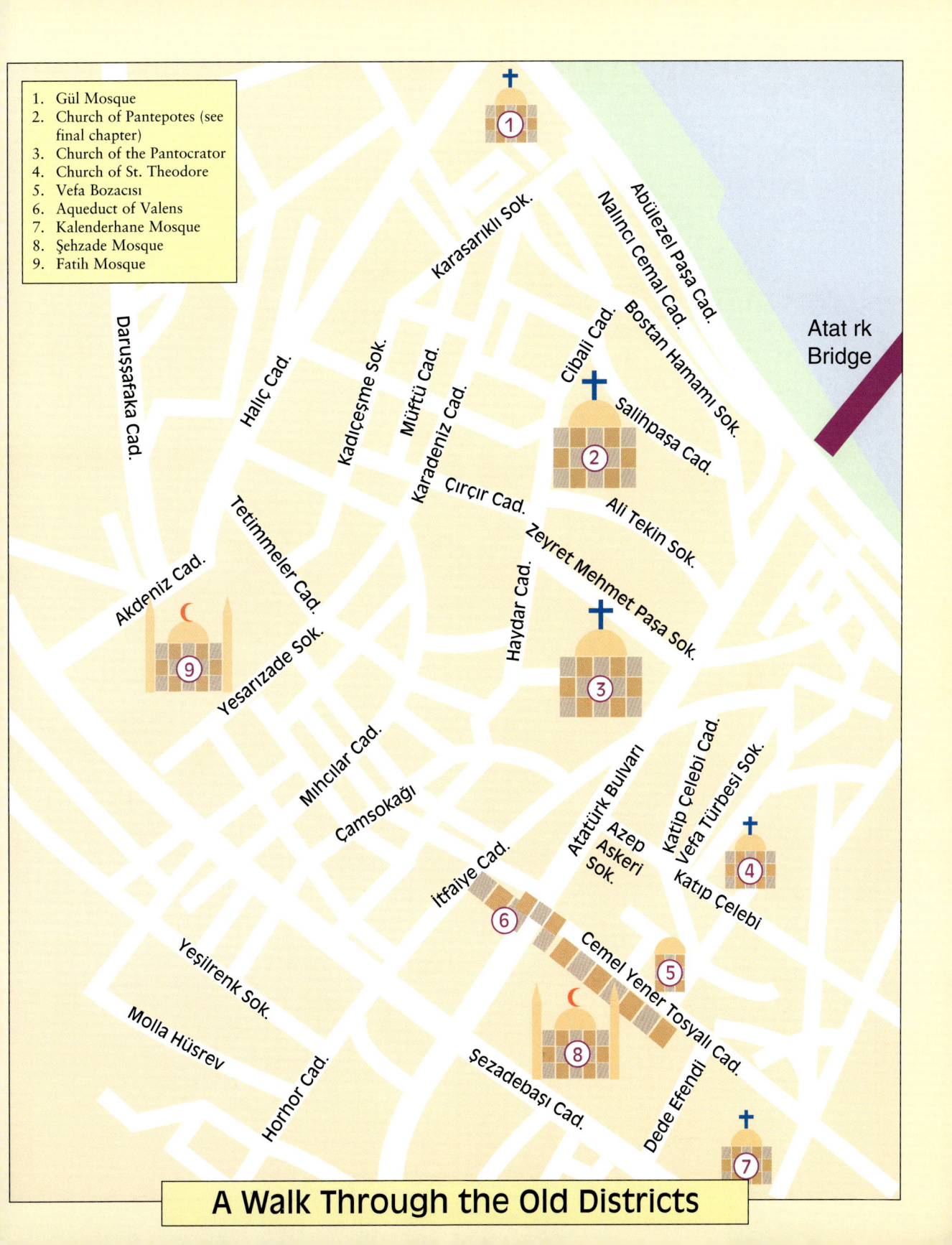

1. Gül Mosque
2. Church of Pantepotes (see final chapter)
3. Church of the Pantocrator
4. Church of St. Theodore
5. Vefa Bozacısı
6. Aqueduct of Valens
7. Kalenderhane Mosque
8. Şehzade Mosque
9. Fatih Mosque

A Walk Through the Old Districts

A Walk Through the Old Districts

Of all the areas described in this book, the line, "to boldly go where no tourist has gone before," surely applies to this walk. Most of the people living in Istanbul hardly know these areas. The churches here are nevertheless imposing and interesting. Strolling through these forgotten parts of town can be very pleasant.

The Gül Mosque

Tucked away in an old neighborhood of Istanbul lies the imposing Church of St. Theodosia, better know as the Gül Camii, or the Mosque of the Roses. The history of this unusual building is very obscure. Grosvenor states in his book—published in 1895—that it is "the ghostliest of Byzantine churches, revealing everywhere the decadence of Byzantine architecture," ascribing it to the last ages of Byzantium. Recent excavations however have shown that this edifice was probably built in the tenth century, during the strong reign of the Macedonian emperors. This is a more logical date than the late thirteenth century when the Byzantines were far too busy with the survival of their tottering Empire to give any concern to the building of lofty churches.

The church was consecrated to Saint Theodosia, a rather zealous nun who could not bear seeing a soldier destroy the beloved icon of Christ above the imperial entranceway of the Palace. Setting her Christian sisterly love aside, she knocked him off the ladder on which he was standing. The unfortunate soldier was killed by the fall and Theodosia was, in turn, executed by his friends who drove a ram's horn down her throat (one must admit, the Byzantines were very inventive in matters of execution). It was the beginning of the iconoclast struggles and from then on the Orthodox church had another martyr. May 29 marked the annual day on which her saintly deed was commemorated. On the day of the conquest of the city (May 29, 1453), a large congregation gathered here to ask for deliverance from the hands of the Turks. The church was decorated with garlands of roses for the occasion, and when the Ottoman soldiers rushed in, they found the roses still in place and that is why the Turks speak of the Gül Camii (Rose Mosque).

The locals say that this church is the final resting place of Constantine XI Dragases, the last Emperor of Byzantium. Although this story has been discredited as mere legend, in fact there is a staircase leading up to a burial chamber. People say that the saintly Gül Baba is buried here, but no one can explain the curious Turkish inscription, *"Tomb of the Apostle, disciple of Jesus, peace be with him."* So there is definitely something mysterious about the church. Under the church are enormous subterranean vaults, and it is said that there is a secret subterranean imperial way to the Hagia Sophia.

Despite the fortress-like exterior of the building, the interior is light and spacious. The mosaic decoration however is gone and the true beauty of the church lies—at least nowadays—in its striking dimensions.

After all these tales of mystery, we now stroll through another old Istanbul neighborhood. Our destination is another church, bigger and even more formidable than the last. We follow the Cibali and Haydar Caddesi and end up at a picturesque square with wooden houses in which the Church of the Pantocrator stands.

The Church of the Pantocrator

This monastery church was built between 1120 and 1136 by John II Comnenus (nicknamed John the Good) and his pious wife the Empress Eirene, whose mosaic portraits are in the Hagia Sophia. The church is the only building that is left from a once vast complex comprising an old people's home, a hospital and a leprosarium (see the chapter on the Hagia Eirene).

Actually the building consists of two churches. The southernmost church (today's mosque) was the earlier. Another church was added later and between them rose, at a slightly later date, a mortuary chapel for the royal Comnenian family.

The brickwork is typical for churches of this time. Seen here is the "recessed" brick masonry type. This is a method by which alternate courses are set back and mortared over. Most likely this was done for decorative purposes, although to some the exterior appears prison-like. Another theory is that this method was used simply as an economical way of using uneven bricks. In any case, the Pantocrator is one of the largest and most interesting churches of the city.

Medieval Byzantine churches, like this one, were never built in the form of a basilica, a rectangular building with a flat roof and/or towers, but always conceived as large centripetal spaces, forcing the gaze toward the dome, the symbol of the cosmos. The dome rests on four columns placed within a square plan. Most unfortunately the red granite columns which once supported the structure are no longer evident as they have been plastered over.

In the 1950s a huge surprise occurred during restoration work with the discovery of a beautiful marble pavement arranged in great squares and circles of colored marbles. Most of this floor is today covered with tatty carpets, but some figural designs are still to be seen.

The chapel, now a mere pigeon-cote, was once called the Heroon, a classical term designating a resting place of a great hero. The name alone suffices to express the formidable ambitions of the Comnenian emperors who were laid to rest here. Nothing is left of the tombs and the lavish decoration. The enamels of the famous Pala d'Oro, the altarpiece of San Marco, came from the Pantocrator, being taken as booty to Venice. The north church is also a sad shell but nonetheless very impressive.

The Church of St. Theodore

There are two more churches and the famous aqueduct of Valens left to discover. A walk down the hill and through the grim underground passage takes us under busy Atatürk Bulvari. From there, it is not very far to the small and lovely twelfth century Byzantine church of St. Theodore, converted into a Moslem place of worship, and now known as Kilise Camii (literally the "Church-Mosque"). The building has an attractive decorated façade and its dome still has a very evident mosaic of the Mother of God surrounded by the prophets. These mosaics resemble those of the Chora Church so probably stem from the early fourteenth century. Some of the columns probably date back to the sixth century. There is much we would like to learn about the history of this little gem but the church is not even mentioned in many written sources.

A Quick Drink at Vefa Bozacısı

Although this is a book on Byzantine history, it would be a pity to ignore the famous Vefa Bozacısı. This venerable Istanbul establishment that opened its doors in 1876 is in the immediate vicinity of the mosque, and nearly always overlooked by tourists. Boza is a drink made from fermented millet.

Vefa Bozacısı
Katip Çelebi Cad 102, Vefa
8:30 - midnight

The Aqueduct of Valens

The aqueduct is attributed to Emperor Valens (364-378) and was built of limestone blocks, probably taken from some other ancient structure. It carried the water from the streams of the Belgrade Forest across the valley between the Fourth and the Third Hill. On the Third Hill, beneath the University Gardens was a large cistern, the *nymphaeum maximum*, from which water was distributed to various part of the city. (No traces of it have yet been found, but the author discovered perhaps an entrance to it, in the basement of an Ottoman han, where he nearly drowned, slipping on the wet stairs, leading down to a dark abyss full of water. A warning for adventurers!)

The original length of the aqueduct was about 1000 meters, today the length is still 920 meters so the best part of it has survived, although it has been repaired on numerous occasions. Its greatest height is 63 meters; the municipality has wisely shut off access to the aqueduct so that it can no longer be climbed.

Maintenance of the aqueduct was neglected during the last ages of the Byzantine Empire. There was simply no longer need for huge amounts of water as the population had dwindled to less than 50,000 inhabitants. In Ottoman times however, the city was repopulated and a shortage of water was soon felt, so subsequent sultans repaired this aqueduct and even built several new ones in the Belgrade Forest.

Kalenderhane Mosque

Just behind the aqueduct lies one of the most beautiful Byzantine churches of the city. The church was built in the late twelfth century and known as the Church of the Holy Mother of God Kyriotissa. At the time of the Latin Conquest of Constantinople (1204-1261), the side chapel was decorated with scenes from the life of St. Francis of Assisi, a most sensational discovery since these frescoes were painted only about 25 years after his death. Sadly enough they are now tucked away in the Archeological Museum and are not displayed. Excavations have revealed a great number of earlier structures on the site, for instance that of a Roman bath and a sixth century basilica.

Although the church has a pretty façade, it is the interior that is captivating. The soft colors of the beautiful marble revetments covering the brick walls evoke a very peaceful atmosphere. The name Kalenderhane is derived from the Kalender Sufi mystics who used the mosque as a *tekke*, a place designated for their religious ceremonies.

Galata

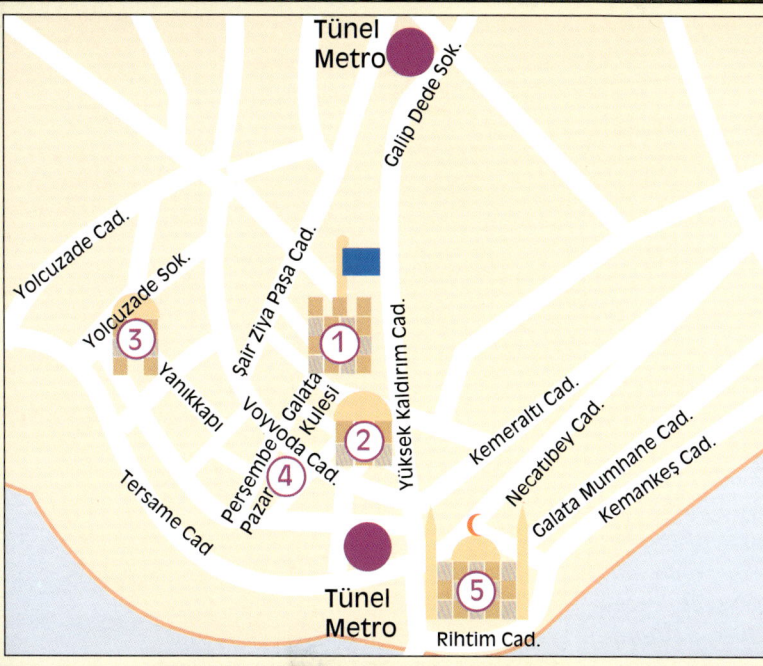

The Golden Horn divides the European part of Istanbul into two parts: the old imperial capital on the right bank and the districts of Galata and Pera (together called Beyoğlu) on the left. This part of town offers a pleasant change in architecture and atmosphere.

1. The Galata Tower
2. Podesta
3. Yanıkkapı
4. 18th Century Ottoman Houses
5. Yeraltı Mosque

History

*I*n antiquity Galata was known as Sycae (the Fig Orchard); by the time of Theodosius (408-450 AD), it was large enough to become the thirteenth ward of the mighty city of Constantinople. According to a statistical account written in the fifth century, The Notitia Urbis Constantinopolitanea, this suburb had 431 houses, a church, a forum, public baths, a theater and—of course—a harbour. It must have been a rather upscale part of town for the Emperor Justinian deemed it important enough to rename it after himself. The name Justinianopolis however didn't stick, and somewhat later this region was called Galata, a name of uncertain origin. The castle of Galata that existed at that time was a fortress built to guard the entrance to the Golden Horn. From there a huge chain was stretched to the opposite shore, closing the Horn in case of attack. The substructures of that building now make up the underground mosque (Yeraltı Camii).

The real history of Galata starts in later Byzantine times and is really more interesting than the obligatory facts that we just mentioned. One has to remember that the final demise of the Byzantines was not only brought about by powerful enemies but also by matters of economy. Of course these factors interacted. Since the military might of the Byzantine armies was not overly impressive, the Comnenian emperors sought to play off the several Italian merchant republics against each other. Being Byzantines, they did this initially quite well, allowing trade concessions first to one, then to the other. When the Empire became weaker and weaker, though, the Venetians and the Genoese fought their battles on Byzantine soil (damaging Greek property as they went along) and drained the revenues of trade. Nicetas Choniates, the palace secretary, complained that they *"became so insolent in their wealth as to hold the imperial power in scorn."* Nevertheless Michael Paleologus (1259-1282) needed their help and in 1267 ceded the whole district of Galata to the Genoese. Of course, he was cunning enough to sign a treaty with archrival Venice the following year, to counterbalance the influence of the Genoese.

Although the Genoese were expressly forbidden to fortify their colony, they soon started building an enceinte. The Tower of Christ (the Galata Tower) is a remainder from this period. The merchants prospered and in his visit to Constantinople in 1344 the Muslim traveler Ibn Battuta reported that the inhabitants of Galata *"are all men of commerce and their harbour is one of the largest in the world; I saw there about a hundred galleys and other large ships, and the small ships were too many to be counted."*

The fortifications were destroyed in 1453, after the conquest. In need of commercial talent, the sultans left the Genoese, who had remained neutral during the siege, where they were. That is why Galata remained, until the last century, a favorite place for foreign trading companies and banks to establish their businesses.

A Walk around Galata

The most imposing structure of the district is the 61-meter high Galata Tower. There are a great number of speculations about early towers that stood on this site but we are sure that the present tower was built in 1348 as the highest part of the walls surrounding the Italian community. The tower was repaired a number of times during the Ottoman era and it is hard to say how much of it is still original. Nowadays there is a restaurant and rather seedy nightclub on top, but the panorama from above is as breathtaking as ever and one of the finest in the city.

The street leading down the hill, the Galata Kulesi Sokağı, is one of the oldest streets in Galata. Walking down, there is a building on the left that is easily recognizable, as it is very much older than the surroundings. It is the *podesta*, the palace of the governor of Galata. The building still has its fourteenth century appearance. Further down the hill are some ancient stone buildings on the right. They are often identified as medieval, but are in fact early eighteenth century Ottoman houses.

The English Hospital

The only surviving gate in the defense wall is located at the bottom of the hill and toward the right at the intersection of Yolcuzade and Yanıkapı Streets. A bronze tablet with the coat of arms of Genoa hangs above the entrance. The Yeraltı Camii (the Underground Mosque) is in the opposite direction toward Karaköy. The sixth century subterranean vaults of the castle of Galata which today houses the mosque are, however, only of historical interest.

The Naval Museum in nearby Beşiktaş displays the huge chain that was stretched from here to the other side. This museum also exhibits the Ottoman galleys. The chain offers a perfect excuse to go and look at these magnificent ships. You will not be disappointed.

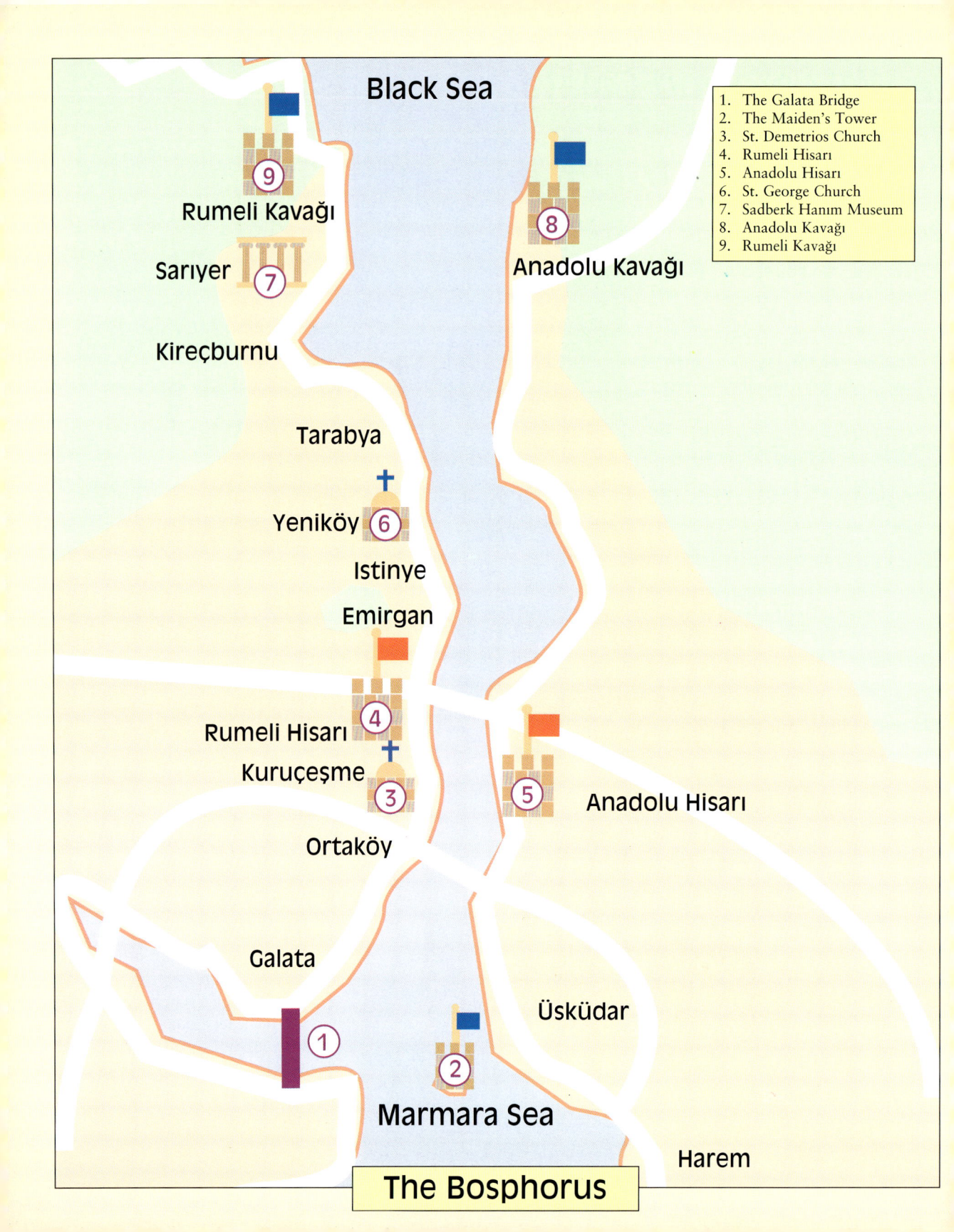

The Bosphorus

Black Sea

1. The Galata Bridge
2. The Maiden's Tower
3. St. Demetrios Church
4. Rumeli Hisarı
5. Anadolu Hisarı
6. St. George Church
7. Sadberk Hanım Museum
8. Anadolu Kavağı
9. Rumeli Kavağı

- Rumeli Kavağı (9)
- Sarıyer (7)
- Kireçburnu
- Anadolu Kavağı (8)
- Tarabya
- Yeniköy (6)
- İstinye
- Emirgan
- Rumeli Hisarı (4)
- Kuruçeşme (3)
- Anadolu Hisarı (5)
- Ortaköy
- Galata
- Üsküdar
- (1)
- (2)
- Harem

Marmara Sea

The Bosphorus

The Bosphorus, the beautiful 31.5 kilometer strait that joins two continents and two seas, has been the subject of numerous myths and legends. Its present name is derived from the myth of Zeus and his mistress Io. Zeus tried to conceal her from his jealous wife by transforming Io into a cow, but Hera was not deceived and provided a horsefly to sting her again and again. To escape, Io plunged into the current and swam across to safety. In ancient Greek *bous* is cow and *poros* is a ford, giving us Bosphorus, the crossing place of the cow. The Byzantines also called the strait Kastastenon, that is the narrows. The Turks seem to have had the same idea for they speak of the Boğaz, or "the throat." Its narrowest point, near the fortress Rumeli Hisarı, is only 800 meters wide.

The Galata Bridge

The Galata Bridge is a good place to enjoy the view and to watch a fleet of ferries toot and whistle across the restless waters of the Bosphorus. The Golden Horn was spanned by a bridge even in Byzantine times, so that, as the chroniclers say, *"one could pass from the other side to the all-happy city."* This bridge must have been located somewhere at its upper end. The sixteenth century French traveler, Gyllius, writes that the stone piers of an ancient bridge could be seen in summer when the water was low, standing opposite a point between the northern extremity of the land walls and Ayvansaray. The name "the Horn" ("Keras" in ancient Greek) is said to be derived from the outline of a deer's antlers formed by the confluence of two streams that run into the upper end of it (in Ottoman times known as the Sweet Waters of Europe). Some versions of the myth of Zeus and Io also say that here, before crossing the Bosphorus, Io gave birth to the nymph Keroessa. From the love of Keroessa and Poseidon was born Byzans of Megara, the founder of Byzantium.

Old Galata

The Maiden's Tower

From the bridge, looking towards the Asian side, a curious little Byzantine tower in the sea is visible. This is the Maiden's Tower (Kız Kulesi), one of Istanbul's landmarks. The Turkish name is derived from a commonplace tale. A fortune teller tells the king that his sweet daughter will die of a snake's bite. The father does everything to protect her and locks her up in the tower, and so on. I leave you to guess the end of the story. People also call it Leander's Tower, from the myth of the unfortunate Leandros who drowned while swimming to his beloved priestess, Hero. Actually this tale belongs to the Dardanelles, but no one seems to care.

In the twelfth century Manuel Comnenos built two strong towers on this islet, as a point of attachment for an iron chain than ran across the Bosphorus from the Asian side to the foot of the Acropolis, where the Topkapı Palace now stands. The tower was rebuilt many times so that there is today nothing Byzantine about it. Nevertheless it is a picturesque building, at least from afar. The famous tower was recently restored in a crude manner and transformed into a rather ghastly cafeteria cum restaurant. There is a regular boat service to the islet.

The Churches of Kuruçesme

The little village of Kuruçesme, on the European Bosphorus shore, is a brief ten-minute taxi ride from Dolmabahçe Palace. The Greek name of the village was Anaplous and this village was the site of several monasteries and palaces. One holy well (*ayazma*) dating to Byzantine times has survived. At the back of the village, up a little flight of stairs, lies the Ayios Demetrios Church. The present-day church was built in 1798, but the church's holy water arrives from a deep cave dating back to the Middle Ages. One can explore the tunnel, drink the curative water and have look at the marble icon of St. Demetrios. The church itself is not of great historical significance but very pretty nonetheless.

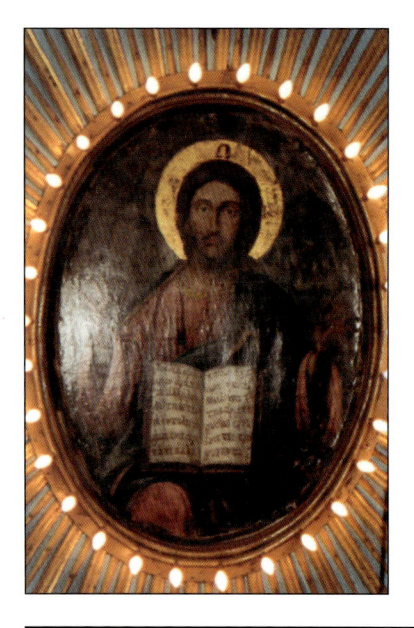

St. Demetrios is one of the most popular military martyrs of the Orthodox church. Like St. Sergius and St. Bacchus of the Küçük Aya Sofya, he was believed to have been a military man who was persecuted under Emperor Diocletian because of his Christians beliefs. He became the patron saint of Thessalonica and "defended" his city against barbarian attack. This is why he is depicted clad in armor with a lance in his hand, trampling a man or a serpent, representing the devil.

Walking back from this church, one sees on the right side another Orthodox church, dedicated to John the Baptist. The building is dated 1835 and is not as lovely as the one just seen.

The Nature of Evil in the Orthodox Church

While sitting in this peaceful church one may reflect on the nature of evil in the Orthodox Church. Unlike Milton's Satan, the Byzantine devil was not a proud rebel, but a rather pathetic figure. He and the other demons were conceived as fallen angels of light, having no existence other than corrupt light. Thus they were easy expelled by the power of radiant truth, as a candle disperses darkness in a room. Despite all his assumed majesty, the devil was powerless. He could not force people and knew no other approach but temptation. Of course temptations were everywhere to be found. There was falsehood, drunkenness, slander, envy, inane speech (including laughter, jokes, obscenity), avarice, sorcery, gluttony, despondency, vanity, idolatry, murder, theft, homosexuality, hardness of heart and so on. The most tempting sins seem to have been adultery and fornication because the Byzantines firmly believed that the great majority of souls on their way to heaven fell into the hands of demons who appealed to this type of behavior. This represents an interesting comment on the pious Byzantine way of life.

Rumeli Hisarı

The fortress of Rumeli Hisarı was built in 1452 and took the bold Sultan Mehmet the Conqueror just four and half months to complete. Since the fortress plays such an important role in Byzantine history it deserves consideration here.

In the spring of 1452 the Byzantines learned that the young Sultan planned to build another fortress at the European side, giving him absolute control of the Bosphorus. An emissary was sent to remind the sultan that his grandfather Beyazıt had at least asked permission when he built his fortress, Anadolu Hisarı, on the opposite Asian shore. The young Sultan had no time for such diplomatic babble and when envoys came for a third time to ask if the Sultan would give his word that Constantinople would not be attacked, he cut off their heads to make clear that he meant business. On April 15 construction started and various churches were torn down to provide building material. By August 31 the building was completed. The Byzantines were now trapped. In November of that year an Italian ship tried to break through the blockade, but was blasted out of the water and the captain impaled on a stake. It horrified the West but still substantial aid did not come. Western princes were much too involved in there own squabbles to intercede, while the Roman Pope looked with suspicion on the heretical Greeks.

The castle with its ivy-covered walls is a very romantic place and is well worth a visit. The upper towers provide an unsurpassed view over the strait. On the opposite shore the little fortress of Anadolu Hisarı built by Sultan Beyazıt in 1391 is visible.

Further up the Bosphorus

After Rumeli Hisarı the road passes through Baltalimanı and Emirgan. The lovely Emirgan Park with its Ottoman mansions is nestled in the hills of Emirgan. In Byzantine days there was a large cypress forest here known as Kyparodes. Cypresses have been associated with eternal life ever since the days of the Ancients because they are always green.

The village of İstinye was called Stenon (narrow). Constantine erected a large basilica here dedicated to the Archangel Michael, who must have been an extremely popular angel because it is known that in Constantinople alone he had no fewer than twenty-four churches. The church was demolished to provide stones for Rumeli Hisarı.

Stenon was also the place where Daniel the Stylite (derived from the Greek for pillar, *stylos*) lived for the best part of his life (409-493). Daniel was an ardent follower of the famous Simeon the Stylite from Syria. The Orthodox Church has always favored ascetics who renounced the convent, as they had renounced the world. The stylites had a little railing around the top and perhaps a tiny roof above their head, but apart from that they were exposed to the scorching heat of summer and the cold of winter. Such incredible ascetic feats of course attracted throngs of believers. So our holy man Daniel was a kind of tourist attraction in those days. Although Daniel spent most of his time in prayer, he did pastoral work too among those who gathered around his column.

The next village Yeniköy (new village) is apparently not so new, since it was called Neapolis by the Byzantines, which has the same meaning as the Turkish name. There is still a little Greek community living in Yeniköy. The present nineteenth century church of St. George (Ayios Yiorgos) has an old graveyard with the tombs of three patriarchs and a holy well. The next town up the Bosphorus, Tarabaya, was famed for its hot springs, but an earthquake long ago seems to have ended their activity. This was and still is a very posh village and the immensely wealthy Phanariote families (see chapter on Fener) built luxurious summer houses here in the eighteenth and nineteenth centuries. Some of their houses are still to be seen although very few Greeks live here nowadays.

From Kireçburnu (formally called Key to the Points because one sees here the first glimpse of the mouth of the Black Sea) the road goes to Büyükdere. This is the widest point of the Bosphorus and the winding waterway seems nearly like a lake here. The Byzantines called this place Kalos Argos (the Beautiful Meadow). A giant plane tree around which the knights of the First Crusade camped in 1096 stood on this meadow, but all beauty is now gone. A little bit further along a beautiful yalı (from the Greek *yialos*, which means "shore") stands at the left hand side of the road. This yalı today houses the Sadberk Hanım Museum. It is the finest private museum of the country and includes an ethnographic section and an archeological wing, with one floor dedicated to Byzantium.

Kireçburnu - The Key to the Points

The Mouth of the Bosphorus

At the top of the strait and on opposite sides of the shore lie the Rumeli and Anadolu Kavakları, former Byzantine toll and custom points. The two villages were connected by an iron chain, supported on rafts, used to prevent ships from passing through the strait without paying their fees.

Above the two hamlets are castles built by the Byzantines. The one on the European side is hardly worth a look, but the one above Anadolu Kavağı is an impressive ruin. It affords a good view over the Bosphorus and the Black Sea. This castle was built in the Paleologian era and then occupied by the Genoese.

The Mouth of the Black Sea

Anadolu Kavağı

Additional Byzantine Monuments and Useful Information

The Church of the Theotokos Pammakaristos

The Church of the All-Blessed Mother of God was once one of the richest churches of the city. It was the burial place of Emperor Alexis Comnenus and his scholarly daughter Anna and important enough to house the Orthodox Patriarchate for a while. In 1568 the church was converted into the Mosque of the Conquest (Fethiye Camii) to celebrate the capture of Georgia and Azerbaijan. The church building consists of two parts. The main body of the church was built somewhere in the twelfth century while the mortuary chapel was added in the early fourteenth century, around the same time that the Chora Church was rebuilt and decorated.

The church has a very pretty exterior and the building is no doubt one of the finest specimens of Byzantine architecture in the city. The chapel with its fine mosaics was meticulously restored in the 1960s by the Byzantine Institute of America. Therefore it is a pity that so much red tape is necessary to gain access. You have to apply at the Hagia Sophia Directorate (the Tourist Office near the Hippodrome might be of some help) and after that you have to wait for a few days and pay $100 for someone to accompany you, and then your group still has to pay entrance fees.

Is it worth it? That depends on how you look at it. If this were another Chora Church then it surely would. In this case you must love Byzantine art because there are not many mosaic panels to be seen. In the dome is—as always—Christ Pantocrator depicted surrounded by twelve Old Testament prophets. In the apse there is another portrait of Christ, flanked by the Theotokos and John the Baptist. Only one of the mosaics that tell the story of Christ survived: the Baptism of Christ. All the other ones are of saints and patriarchs and probably only of interest to the specialists.

The church is located on Fethiye Caddesi and locals will help you find it. From here you can walk to the lovely church of Mary of the Mongols, described in the chapter on Fener.

The Church of St. John Stoudion

*I*t is only a five minute walk from the Yedikule railway station to this very ancient and important church, the only true basilica in the city. Again one has to ask for permission in advance at the Hagia Sophia directorate. The door is firmly locked but you can scale the walls of the apse in order to get a good look at the fine interior of this building.

This church was founded in 463, not long after the Theodosian walls were completed. The nearby monastery (now gone) was inhabited by the order of the Akoimetoi, the sleepless ones, who, divided into three groups, prayed and chanted day and night. The monks were known for their vigorous lives, their severe mortification, their strict discipline and their rigorous fasts. We are told that not even female animals were allowed within its precincts.

This monastery was however not only a place of prayer but an important intellectual center as well. The monks were obliged to spend their time studying and copying evangels and historical works. During the first half of the fifteenth century the Patriarchal Academy was located here. This institution was so widely respected that it even drew students from Italy. It was a place that attracted many pilgrims, too, since the head of St. John the Baptist was preserved here. The Emperor himself attended service here on the Feast of Decapitation (August 29).

The church was a timber-roofed basilica with three aisles separated by columns supporting a horizontal entablature. You can see all this if you peek through the large windows of the apse. Parts of the splendid decorative marble floor are still to be seen and from above you can gain even a better impression of it.

From this church you can have a nice walk along the sea walls and through picturesque areas with lots of wooden houses and kitchen gardens. If you take the road behind the basilica that leads downhill, you will come to the railway line. If you follow the tracks, you will eventually get to Samatya, an area that was in Ottoman times a predominately Greek and Armenian district. There are many small sixteenth to nineteenth century churches to be found here, but none of them are of great historical interest.

Walking from the little village square, with its many *meyhanes* (Greek style tavernas), to the main street (Samatya Caddesi) brings into view the tall bell tower of the nineteenth century Church of St Menas. Beneath it is the oldest mausoleum of all Istanbul, the Martyrium of the Holy Karpos and Papylos. The round brick chamber which today functions as a carpentry shop is very impressive and must date back at least to the fourth century.

Some Other Churches around the City

Bodrum Mosque
A tenth century Byzantine church is located in the heart of Aksaray among its rather depressing concrete buildings. Today this former church is called the Bodrum Mosque. It was built in 922 by Emperor Romanus I Lecapenus as a part of his palace. The building was restored in a disastrous manner in 1965. Ninety percent of the exterior masonry was then replaced with concrete bricks. Underneath the building (hence the name Bodrum meaning "basement") is a vast Roman rotunda dating back to the fifth century. Its purpose is unknown but it was used as a cistern in later times. Today it houses a very seedy shopping mall.

The Church of St. Saviour Pantepotes
In the vicinity of the Pantocrator Church, about a five minute walk, but rather hard to find, stands the Eski İmaret Mosque, the former Church of Christ the All-Seeing. The tiny church with its nice brick façade was founded or restored by Anna Dalassenes, mother of Alexius Comnenus I (1081-1118).

The Fenari İsa Mosque
A large church known as the Monastery of Constantine Lips was built by its namesake, a high ranking bureaucrat at the court of Leo the Wise. He built the north church in 908 and dedicated it to the Theotokos Panachrantos, the Immaculate Mother of God. This is one of the oldest Byzantine churches in the city and must have been quite an important edifice because several members of the Paleologian dynasty were buried here. Excavations have revealed a number of tombs and two imperial sarcophagi. The monastery church stands nowadays on the busy Adnan Menderes Bulvari (until recently Vatan Caddesi), the major traffic way leading to Topkapı Gate. The building burned a number of times so that it is more or less a miracle that it has survived the onslaught of time.

Practical Information

Opening times

Hagia Sophia: open every day, except Monday, from 09.30 - 16.30.

Basilica Cistern (Yerebatan Saray): open every day from 09.30 - 17.30.

The Mosaic Museum (Great Palace): open every day, except Monday, from 09.30 - 16.30. (But you can try to sneak in on Monday, as they are always open.)

Chora Museum (Kariye Camii): open every day, except Wednesday, from 09.30 - 16.30.

Yedikule (Fortress of Seven Towers): open every day, except Wednesday, from 09.30 - 16.30. (Officially that is, most of the time the gate keeper is there after closing time.)

Museum of Sadberk Hanım (on the Bosphorus): open every day, except Wednesday, from 10.00 - 17.30.

Archeological Museum: open every day, except Monday, from 09.30 - 16.30.

Further Reading

By far the most enjoyable and thrilling account on the history of the Byzantine Empire was written by John Julius Norwich. The three volume set is available in Penguin paperback. Norwich also wrote an abridged version of his history in one volume, also available at Penguin.

The nester of Byzantine scholarship, Steven Runciman, wrote a host of books on the Byzantine Empire. Very accessible is *Byzantine Style and Civilisation* (Penguin). A detailed account of the conquest of the city is to be found in *The Fall of Constantinople*. *The Byzantine Theocracy* (Cambridge University Press) deals with the relationship between Church and State. A very recommendable book is also *The Great Church Captivity* (Cambridge University Press), which deals with the less well-known subject of the Church's survival during Ottoman Rule.

An easy, readable book about women in Byzantine society is Donald M. Nicol's *The Byzantine Lady. Ten portraits 1250-1500*. On the topic of gender you could also read *Women, Men, Eunuchs*, by James Liz (editor) (Routledge 1997).

If you want to read something that is written in Byzantine times, there is no better choice than *Fourteen Byzantine Rulers* of Michael Psellus, a vivid account of the court life in the 11th century. Another interesting choice is the *Alexiad*, the biography of the Byzantine Emperor Alexius I (1081-1118) by his daughter Anna Comnena. The book famously records the fearful entry into Constantinople of the First Crusade. Both are published in paperback by Penguin.

There are numerous books in the field of art. The books by Talbot Rice and Andre Grabar can make at times very dull reading. I would recommend therefore: *Byzantine Art* by Robin Cormack (Oxford University Press) or *The Art of Byzantine* by Thomas F. Mathews (The Every Man Art Library). Both books are well illustrated, scholarly, but easygoing.

An excellent author who covers many aspects of Byzantium and has written many books on Byzantine art and culture is Cyril Mango. A good introduction is *Byzantium, the Empire of New Rome* (Phoenix Giant).

Internet sources:

Many of the books you might want to acquire are likely to be sold out or very expensive. With the ABEbook and the Bibliofind search engines you can find nearly every book and often at bargain prices.

At http://www.byzantium1200.org you can see scale models of the different monuments. Some of the models however don't look very authentic to me but more like neo-classical buildings.

One of the best web sites on recent excavations carried out in Constantinople is provided by the University of Illinois, http://www.arch.uiuc.edu. A wealth of information can also be found at the Constantinople Home Page, http://www.bway.net/~halsall.

About the Author:

Robert van den Graven (1962), studied history and philosophy in the Netherlands. He fell in love with Istanbul as a student and has been coming back ever since. Today he works as an antiquarian bookseller specializing in the Near East, while also teaching at the University and organizing cultural tours to Istanbul. If you need any help or want to join one of his tours please contact him at konstantinopel@hotmail.com.